THE BEAUTIFUL WORK
OF LEARNING TO PRAY

THE
BEAUTIFUL
WORK

OF
LEARNING
TO
PRAY

31 Lessons

James C. Howell

Abingdon Press
Nashville

Library of Congress Cataloging--in-Publication Data

Howell, James C., 1955-
The beautiful work of learning to pray : 31 lessons / James C. Howell.
  p. cm.
Includes index.
ISBN 0-687-02766-7
1. Prayer—Christianity. I. Title.

BV215.H69 2003
248.3'2—dc21

2003002556

03 04 05 06 07 08 09 10 11 12 — 10 9 8 7 6 5 4 3 2 1

MANUFACTURED IN THE UNITED STATES OF AMERICA

In Memory of
Mama and Papa Howell

CONTENTS

Introducing Prayer

Back in the fourth century, St. Ephrem wrote,

Let our prayer be a mirror, Lord, placed before Your
face;
then Your fair beauty will be imprinted on its luminous surface.

Prayer is our pursuit of beauty. Prayer is beautiful. But
prayer is elusive, not easily won. When we talk about
prayer, we inevitably say contradictory things. Prayer is
natural, prayer is our life, prayer is like breathing. Yet at the
same time, prayer is hard, prayer is like a foreign language,
prayer is frustrating. Prayer is a free gift God gives to everyone, and yet it is understood thoroughly by very few.

This book sets a course by which you might grow in the
life of prayer. You could explore these thirty-one lessons
daily for a month, or at any pace that fits who and where
you are. Some lessons will state the obvious, while others
will pose stiff challenges. When we try to pray, we bump up

against frustrations and barriers. In this book we will talk about how we grapple with these inevitable difficulties. Our desire is to get beyond a superficial, unsatisfying prayer life, and to begin to discover the fullness of prayer, silence, praise, giving thanks, confession, feelings, the Bible and prayer, love, praying together, hearing God's calling, disciplines, and hopefulness in prayer.

Learning to pray should be something profound and mysterious, yet learning to pray is utterly practical, and over a lifetime of praying you pick up a hint here, a simple suggestion there. For prayer is something we practice. Prayer is a skill to be developed. I will pass along prayers you can actually pray, samples from wise pray-ers who knew (or know) God more intimately than you and I do. But remember: nobody gets to be an expert in prayer. We are all of us amateurs.

When I think of learning to pray, I remember taking piano lessons as a child. When I turned six, my mother decreed that I would learn to play. The rudiments of piano are boring, repetitive, and I expended considerable energy before I could feebly struggle through "Mary Had a Little Lamb" in my first recital. But we kept going, for years. Most days I could think of dozens of activities that would be more fun. Boys in the neighborhood would laugh, or call me a "sissy." Every day at the appointed time I would practice, though, and I got better. Notes yielded to scales, which yielded to chords, and before long I was playing Beethoven, Mozart, and Chopin.

You cannot learn to play by yourself. You need a teacher, a master, a veteran who knows the music and the skills required. In this book we will frequently quote the words of saints—heroes in prayer—for they yearn to be our teachers.

Pianists (and those who listen to them) are delighted when a pair of magical moments finally manifest themselves. For years you work and practice, and you try to get the notes right. But then, through some barely detectable movement of grace, you get the feel of the music, and instead of just playing notes, you are playing the song itself, sensing its pulse, voicing its soul. And you are proud, and listeners applaud.

But there is more. You keep practicing, you play more songs, and then one day, mysteriously, you become so lost in the music that you no longer are performing the music so others can hear. You become the listener. Yes, you're still the one sitting there, you're the possessor of the fingers moving about the keyboard. But in your soul you aren't playing so much as you too are listening, delighting in the music, even delighting in the composer, who may be long since in the grave, but lives in the lovely moment of the music coming to expression.

Prayer is even better than the joyful brilliance of a master pianist. The first tentative notes are gathered up by a loving God who hangs on our every word, just as parents root for their six-year-old in a recital of "Mary Had a Little Lamb." Yet prayer is in the learning, in the practicing. Praying more often enables you to pray more. The more you enjoy the prayer, the more you sense the melody, the harmonies of God's gracious presence, until finally you are "lost in wonder, love, and praise," and your prayer isn't something you do, but prayer becomes the exuberant enjoyment of the Composer of the universe, of our lives. And age and feebleness, even death itself, cannot take prayer away from us, for our eternal destiny is nothing other than prayer itself. And it is beautiful.

So let us begin this beautiful work of prayer.

BEGINNING

In the beginning was the Word.   *—John 1:1*

We begin our conversations on prayer. To some devout people, prayer is as natural as breathing. But to many modern people, prayer seems alien and futile. If you are bothering to read this, you probably are at least hopeful that there is such a thing as prayer, that there is a God on the other end, and that a meaningful relationship can happen.

Gazing across the centuries, we notice that prayer is pretty normal. About 50,000 years ago, when anthropologists say our ancestors' brain size began to expand and human beings came into their own, painted art began to appear on caves indicating religious belief. When human consciousness "woke up," there was born simultaneously—like a twin in the soul—an impulse to transcend earthly consciousness, and to connect with a power beyond. Humans have always yearned for something beyond ourselves, beyond this world. Primitive people prayed for rain, and fell on their knees when the crops ripened.

As our brains have gotten bigger and smarter, we have begun to shed our sense of dependence upon God. We have come to think of ourselves as masters of the universe, as arbiters of our own fate. In a smarter world, prayer has become confused and pushed to the margins of life.

But prayer is not contrary to intelligence. Perhaps prayer requires (or is!) a deeper intelligence. One thing we must recognize: prayer is not a way of getting a grip on our lives, of getting things under control. Prayer is the yielding of control. Prayer is discovering I am not the center of the universe, that God is working in hidden yet certain ways. Prayer is realizing we have a relationship with a good and loving God. Prayer is our openness to getting involved in God's adventure with us in the world.

Prayer is hard in our world, but prayer is possible—and desperately needed. Our hollowness, our cynicism, our hopelessness, these are signs from God who is crying out to us, encouraging us to reach out to God, to talk, to listen. We are more than flesh and blood. There is a mystery in my heart, and in yours, a mystery bigger than myself. Hans Urs von Balthasar wrote that each of us "is built like a tabernacle around a most sacred mystery. . . . This sanctuary is neglected and forgotten, like an overgrown tomb or an attic choked with rubbish, and it needs an effort . . . to clean it up and make it habitable. . . . But the room itself does not need to be built: it is already there."

And so let us begin by praying together: Lord, I do not know how to pray. My heart is hidden even from myself. But my heart is not hidden from you. I will need considerable help to clean the place up. Yet I will work energetically, expecting that you are there waiting for me, and for all of us, to come home. O Lord, teach us to pray. *Amen.*

CLOSER THAN WE THINK

We do not know how to pray as we ought.   *—Romans 8:26*

A twofold premise of these lessons is that (a) prayer isn't easy, but also that (b) prayer can be learned. Some of us learned "bedtime" prayers as children ("Now I lay me down to sleep..."). Certainly throughout life we need to retain something of a childlike, simple, trusting approach to prayer. But usually as the rest of my "self" grows up, I need for my prayers to grow up as well, to become more mature. And as an adult, there is generally nobody there to remind you, "Now let's bow our heads and say our prayers."

Prayer is difficult, and we will diagnose some of the reasons (such as our busyness, all the noise, an inability to concentrate). Yet for me there are two kinds of comfort, two hopeful thoughts, hidden in the difficulties.

1. Sometimes we see somebody who seems to be a stalwart at prayer, some beaming, smiling paragon of spirituality whose soul appears to have a direct, fast-access line to heaven. To me, such people are discouraging. We need examples of *how* to pray! But it is paradoxically encouraging to discover that even the greatest saints of the Church have struggled with their prayer life. Some of Mother Teresa's letters have been published, revealing her struggles in prayer. For instance, she wrote, "I am told God lives in me, and yet the reality of darkness and coldness and emptiness is so great that nothing touches my soul." And, "Where I try to raise my thoughts to heaven, there is such convicting emptiness that those very thoughts return like sharp knives and hurt my very soul."

So we are never alone in our struggle, which leads to a more important truth:

2. Prayer isn't easy, but that doesn't mean God isn't there. The barriers to prayer are all on our side, and God is always thrashing at them, always drawing as close to us as our next breath. You can trust in this: When God seems most absent, God is surprisingly most present. Listen to Oscar Romero, the heroic archbishop of El Salvador, in a sermon preached on Good Friday one year before he was assassinated in 1980:

"God is not failing us when we don't feel his presence. Let's not say: God doesn't do what I pray for so much, and therefore I don't pray anymore. God exists, and he exists even more, the farther you feel from him. God is closer to you when you think he is farther away and doesn't hear you. When you feel the anguished desire for God to come near because you don't feel him present, then God is very close to your anguish. When are we going to understand that God not only gives happiness, but also tests our faithfulness in moments of affliction? It is then that prayer and religion have most merit: when one is faithful in spite of not feeling the Lord's presence. Let us learn from that cry of Christ that God is always our Father and never forsakes us, and that we are closer to him than we think."

A meaningful life of prayer is closer than you think. Romans 8:26 does not merely say, "We do not know how to pray as we ought." Paul also says, "The Spirit helps us in our weakness." This is our hope.

So we pray together: Lord, I do not know how to pray as I ought. I feel far from you. Thank you for refusing ever to be far from me. I am encouraged knowing that I am closer to you than I have imagined. I am not alone, and we are not alone. You are always with me, with us. O Lord, teach us to pray. *Amen.*

BARRIERS TO PRAYER

You are worried and distracted by many things. —Luke 10:41 NRSV

There may be as many barriers to prayer as there are people trying to pray. You probably have a particular challenge in praying that you would rank number one, for we are all uniquely gifted, but also uniquely challenged in the life of prayer.

Henri Nouwen, in a great little book on the spiritual life called *With Open Hands*, reminds us that "the resistance to praying is like the resistance of tightly clenched fists." He tells of a woman in a psychiatric center who swung wildly at everyone until they had to restrain her and take everything from her. It took two people to pry open her hand, to find one small coin that she refused to yield, as if she would lose her self if she let go of that coin. Prayer is hard, because it is like letting go. We hang on to what is familiar, even if it's of no great value. But, "each time you dare to let go and surrender one of those many fears, your hand opens a little and your palms spread out in a gesture of receiving."

We hang desperately on to our "busyness," which is a devious culprit ruining our life with God. Why do we get so busy? Are we victims? Or are we more responsible for being busy than we'd like to admit? The world tells me: "It's all up to you! You've got to make it happen, to charge ahead." My calendar weighs on me like some albatross—but my calendar also props up my illusion that I am somebody. Like Atlas, we hoist the world on our shoulders.

But the world wears us out. It's too big. Only God can handle the world. A clenched fist works, fights, grabs, holds on—but as Frederick Buechner put it, "The one thing a clenched fist cannot do is accept...a helping hand."

Prayer begins when we admit we need help. I love this humorous remark from Isaac Bashevis Singer: "I only pray when I am in trouble. But I am in trouble all the time." All the time you and I are incapable of being God. All the time we are in more trouble than we can imagine.

All the time we are asked to swallow lies about time. Bill Gates doesn't go to church, for he views religion as an inefficient use of time. Prayer is wasting time. Wasting time with God. Jesus never said, "Blessed are the efficient, for they will be productive." We have to open our clenched fists that hang desperately on to the illusion that we must cram our time full, that more is better, than who I am is defined by what I do, by what I produce.

To waste time with God requires a reorientation of our whole being. It requires some practice, training, and discipline. Our culture peppers us with sound bites, little clips of noise. Prayer invites us to be still, to be quiet, to concentrate—but our body will rebel against us, as our adrenaline just keeps pumping, so addicted are we to stress.

At first, being still, wasting time with God, and opening our hands may ravage us with painful withdrawal symptoms. Everything will scream, "Get moving again! Tighten that fist!" But we remember we are in trouble. There is this gaping hole in the marrow of my soul. For too long I've been, as Kathy Mattea sings, "knee-deep in a river, and dying of thirst."

The only way to pray is, simply, to pray. And the only way to pray well, the only way to move more deeply into the life of prayer, is to pray more, to pray much.

And so, let us pray: O Lord, I am too busy. I am overcommitted, which means I have a hard time being committed at all. In the midst of rushing about, I miss you. I am in trouble all the time. I cannot fathom letting go of my familiar life. I cannot fathom wasting time and feeling okay about it. I cannot fathom being still. I cannot fathom a new image of my self. But you see me as your child. You can calm my fears. You are my helping hand, our helping hand. You alone can quench my thirst. Help me learn practical ways to let you lift me up, and all of us up, into your loving arms. O Lord, teach us to pray. *Amen.*

COLDNESS

O LORD, you are behind and before me. You lay your hand upon me. . . . If I take the wings of the morning, even there your right hand shall hold me. —*Psalm 139:4-5, 9-10 A.T.*

The obvious barriers to prayer are our busyness, time constraints, all the racket of the world, a simple lack of experience, feeling "nobody is in this with me." Two others seem to me to be important.

One is self-image. Prayer is muddied when my subconscious keeps nagging me by asking, "Why would God talk to *me*?" Sure, others can pray, others are close to God, others have important things. Why would God listen to me?

A corroded self-image plagues everything we do in life. Beginning in childhood, and increasing into adulthood, toxins get dumped into your soul that can make you feel small, ridiculous, unworthy.

But the beauty of the gospel is that the love of God is for everyone, whether you are tall or short, old or young, poor or rich, optimistic or pessimistic, sunny or gloomy, happy or sad, whether you are a spiritual giant or the would-be toddler who can't get organized for even the first step.

Perhaps prayer can be more alive for the toddler, because the spiritual giant's gigantic spirituality can be the most insidious barrier to prayer. Jesus responded tenderly to children, to sick old women, to demon-ravaged young men, to tax collectors and hookers, but harshly to the very pious Pharisees, whose mountainous spiritual self-esteem focused their attention on their mountainous "self" instead of on God.

The principle of prayer is like pictures children color: there are no bad pictures, and you are encouraged to color outside the lines. You are God's child, so you take up your crayon and express yourself to a God who is curled inside your own hand, nudging you along, eager to see what's next.

This leads to a second ironic kind of barrier. Quite rightly, we are skittish about what might actually happen if we pray—which jumps ahead to the notion that prayer isn't just me talking to God, but God talking to me. We have this sneaking suspicion that, were I really to listen to God, I would have to change some things. Maybe lots of things. For my life is out of order, my priorities are out of whack.

The paradox is once more that with clenched fist we cling to an old two-bit life because it is familiar, when God is inviting us to a newer, richer, fuller life. Thomas Merton was right: "Much of our coldness and dryness in prayer may well be a kind of unconscious defence against grace."

Most certainly, prayer will make change necessary. Prayer at the same time will seduce you toward change. Prayer will enable change. Prayer will invite you to some major spring cleaning of your soul. And you shouldn't have a yard sale, for the stuff you've hung on to isn't good for anybody else either, so just trash it.

Prayer may feel like some surgery you would rather postpone, but prayer cannot begin until you've decided that in your deepest self you want a different life, a richer life. You refuse to go on as is. You want the tenderness of God's grace to be as fresh as the air you breathe.

Grace is the hardest for us to receive, so schooled are we at working and earning. But grace is the free gift from the universe—undeserved, undeservable.

So we pray. The only way to pray is to pray. We grow to accept grace. We will not be left in the cold. Pray for the desire to pray, for a willingness for whatever might be in God's future for us.

And so we pray together: Lord, why you would have the time and passion for me way down here escapes me. But I believe that I cannot escape you. I have tried to elude your claim on my life, sometimes even when I am being religious. But I believe I cannot escape you, and I don't even want to. I am thirsty for you, for your grace. O Lord, teach us to pray. *Amen.*

PRAY AS YOU CAN

When you pray, go into your room and shut the door. —*Matthew 6:6*

So. What are some very practical hints to help us pray? First, relax a little. You may be praying already more than you realize. Frederick Buechner suggests:

"Everybody prays whether he thinks of it as praying or not. The odd silence you fall into when something very beautiful is happening or something very good or bad. The ah-h-h! that sometimes floats up out of you. . . . The stammer of pain at somebody else's pain. The stammer of joy at somebody else's joy. Whatever words or sounds you use for sighing with over your own life. These are all prayers in their way. These are all spoken not just to yourself but to something more familiar than yourself."

Prayer builds on these moments, these instincts, and it is important to structure your life and space in ways that maximize the possibilities for you to sigh over your life, and over God.

There is no one way to pray. You must develop your own rituals, and these can even shift during a lifetime. Don't try to make it hard. Pray as you can, not as you can't.

Do not be bludgeoned by some image of what prayer ought to be. Maybe your grandmother prayed in a way you envy. But you're not your grandmother. Know yourself, what invigorates you, what sucks life from you. Susan Howatch wrote that hell is "being obliged to pretend to be someone quite other than one's true self." Prayer will never work if you pretend to be somebody else. Pray as you can, not as you can't.

Be pragmatic about prayer. Where is it quiet? comfortable? When is there a lower likelihood of interruptions? Do you have a chair that might be comfortable, but not too comfortable? Can you dedicate some place in your home or office for prayer, a corner, a little nook? Are there pictures you might put there, of a spiritual hero, of Christ, of a scene in nature? Can you shut the door?

I know a woman who prays as she irons, each swath being a supplication to God. You may pray as you jog, praying for people in each home you pass. Prayer may work best when you are in your pajamas with a cup of coffee, or you may wrap a shawl around your shoulders late at night. Folding laundry, walking the dog, in line at the grocery store—there are countless little occasions for little prayers, and getting into the habit of praying can transform otherwise dull or trying busyness into glimpses of the goodness of God in real life.

How can you communicate with God? Ask how you communicate most freely in the rest of your life! I talk out loud, and so I frequently pray out loud (better done in the car than in the grocery store, where people will think you're a lunatic). Some people write their prayers. Some actually write a letter: "Dear God, There is so much I've been meaning to tell you..." Some read the prayers of others, and make them their own. Some use e-mail: create some e-mail address for God, and peck away. Pray as you can, not as you can't.

Attend to your body when you pray. Notice your breathing. Relax your shoulders (and I'll bet they're tensed up from the stress of your day). Use your imagination. I know a woman who says that her prayer time is her "lap time." Like a little child, she imagines climbing into her father's lap, just to be there, to be held, loved, cradled.

You may be tense or nervous. But remember: prayer is like the world's largest yet most intimate AA meeting. You're unsure you want to be there, but you know you need to be there, so you begin: "My name is James, and I am a sinner." Or: "My name is James, and I have this horribly dark hole in the place where my heart ought to be." Or: "My name is James, I am addicted to the futility of my life." Or: "My name is James, and I am thirsty." Or: "My name is James, and I am so happy to be home in my Father's lap."

If your mind wanders, don't panic or feel guilty. Let your mind wander, and let God gather those wanderings into your prayer. If my mind wanders to the meeting I'm headed to, then I catch myself, and pray about that meeting. If my mind gravitates toward the dinner menu I'm about to cook, I let that meal, and my family and guests who are to eat the meal, become faces in my prayer.

So we pray together: Lord, help me assess my schedule, my space, my posture, my routine, my personality, and show me how to pray as I can. For you are more familiar than my own face, than my own breathing. The room you have made in my soul, in my life, is there. I will go there, and close the door, and feel after your presence. O Lord, teach us to pray. *Amen.*

L E S S O N   S I X

TIME

For everything there is a season . . . a time to seek . . . a time to keep silence . . .
a time to love . . . . He has made everything beautiful in its time.
— Ecclesiastes 3:1-11

In the last lesson, we spoke of helpful hints, practical ways to make prayer easier. But the harder truth is this: in order to pray, you must (not "may need to" but "must") commit what may be our most precious treasure— *time.*

To have a relationship with God, you must get serious about structuring your time, reflecting on its meaning, and dedicating time to the relationship with God that simply will not happen without time, any more than a friendship or marriage can happen without time. We are capable of structuring time to make things happen, like exercise, or being in a club, making a tee time, showing up for dinner. We are capable of structuring time for prayer.

Think of your body's schedule. Are you alert and imaginative in the morning? or are you like me, in a fog before 9 A.M.? If you are weary and drowsy at 11 P.M., that's probably not a good time for prayer. Later we will examine why beginning and ending every day with prayer makes sense, but for the focus of our prayer, we need to find a time that our bodies and souls are inclined to reach out, to be reached.

For prayer to happen, people around you will need to honor and respect that time. Tell your spouse you need the hour between eight and nine to pray, which means he won't plead with you to "Come watch this show!" or "Let's go play golf!" She won't turn the stereo up or sigh about errands undone. Spouses, friends, and siblings show their love for you when they say, "I will give you the space, turn off the TV, whatever it takes, for I value your spiritual self and will help you to love God."

Henri Nouwen, one of my heroes in the spiritual life, admitted he struggled with time for years, until a mentor, John Eudes, told him:

"The only solution is a prayer schedule that you will never break. . . . Set a time that is reasonable, and once it is set, stick to it at all costs. Make it your most important task. Let everyone know that this is the only thing you will not change and pray at that time. . . . Leave a party when that time approaches. Simply make it an impossibility to do any type of work, even if it seems urgent, important, and crucial. When you remain faithful, you slowly discover that it is useless to think about your many problems since they won't be dealt with in that time anyhow. Then you start saying to yourself, 'Since I have nothing to do now, I might just as well pray!' So praying becomes as important as eating and sleeping, and the time set free for it becomes a very liberating time to which you become attached....

"In the beginning...your thoughts will wander, but after while you will discover that it becomes easier to stay quietly in the presence of the Lord. . . . Because in this useless hour in which you do nothing "important" or "urgent," you have to come to terms with your basic powerlessness, you have to feel your fundamental inability to solve your or other people's problems or to change the world. When you do not avoid that experience but live through it, you will find out that your many projects, plans, and obligations become less urgent, crucial, and important and lose their power over you."

And so we pray together: O Lord, time feels like an enemy. I get sucked into feeling I don't have time to pray. Remind me that I cannot afford not to pray, that being with you is more important than eating or exercise, for you are my breath, my bread, my drink, my love. Do not let me be slack about my time, O Lord, and persist until I block out time for you, for I know then I will discover your presence in the rest of my time, which really is your time. O Lord, teach us to pray. *Amen.*

WHAT IS IN US

Cast all your cares on God, for God cares for you.   —*1 Peter 5:7 A.T.*

A presupposition of our series of lessons is that we need to learn to pray, to broaden, to deepen our prayer life, even to reorient why we pray in the first place. Back in the third century, Origen taught that we should think of prayer not as a way to gain some benefit, but rather as a means to become more like God.

While we may seek instruction in prayer, and while we certainly desire to be changed by our prayer, we begin so very simply by opening the heart. Prayer is the exposure of your self to God. Prayer is honesty. Honesty may be hard, for we may prefer to hide parts of our selves from God.

But C. S. Lewis is right that in prayer "we must lay before Him what is in us, not what ought to be in us." We may wonder, "Is it okay to pray for this, or that?" or "How could this little issue be of concern to God?" But everything in me is of concern to God. God cares for every nook and cranny of my life and your life, even more than we care for ourselves. We hide nothing, and we do not need to hide anything. Whatever is going on, whatever is in your heart, the best and only place to cast all those cares is upon God, who cares for you.

Somebody may try to finesse things and suggest what you can or can't pray. Madeleine L'Engle tells of the long weekend while she and her husband waited for a biopsy result. She kept praying, "Please, dear God, don't let it be cancer." Someone suggested that her prayer was invalid: the tumor already either was or wasn't malignant. But she said, "I can't live with that. . . . I think the heart overrides the intellect and insists on praying. . . . If we don't pray according to the needs of the heart, we repress our deepest longings. . . . And so I pray as my heart needs to pray." Later, after the cancer was pronounced terminal, she wondered if her prayers had been wasted. But she concluded, rightly:

"Prayer is love, and love is never wasted. . . . Surely the prayers have sustained me, are sustaining me. Perhaps there will be unexpected answers to these prayers, answers I may not even be aware of for years. But they are not wasted. They are not lost. I do not know where they have gone, but I believe that God holds them, hands outstretched to receive them like precious pearls."

If we lay before God what is in us, all that is in us, then our prayers must be more than 9-1-1 prayers of panic, and our prayer "list" will include far more than people we know who are sick. We will offer up our feelings, our fears, our dreams, our jobs, our anxieties, our little delights, our dark habits, our loves and our pet peeves, all into the loving, healing, hopeful presence of God. To learn to pray, we begin by praying what is in us, not just what we think ought to be in us.

And so we pray together: O Lord, I want above all else to be known, by somebody. I want that somebody to be you. I find it hard to be totally honest, even with myself. Free me up to be totally honest with you, to explore the inner recesses of my mind, heart, and life, for I know you are there, ready to listen, full of care. O Lord, teach us to pray. *Amen*.

BRUISED KNUCKLES

Knock, and the door will be opened to you. — *Luke 11:9 A.P.*

George Buttrick once described prayer as beating on heaven's door "with bruised knuckles in the dark"—which perfectly captures the seeming frustration of prayer, and the persistence required if we are to pray. In Luke 11:5-13, Jesus tells of a man banging on his friend's door at midnight, demanding bread. Rebuffed at first, he persists. He will not be denied. Persistence in prayer will be hard for us in our "quick" culture, where speed and efficiency are everything, where we press a button and stuff gets delivered to our doors. Prayer is not quick. Prayer is not efficient. Communion with God isn't won in fifteen seconds.

Back to banging on the door. Jesus, obviously talking about prayer, concludes, "Ask and it will be given you . . . ," — words that are simultaneously hopeful and discouraging. Hopeful, for our beating on heaven's door will not finally be ignored. Discouraging though, for Jesus makes it sound as if prayer "works," and I know what you know, that very often our prayers seem to fall uselessly down to the floor, never having penetrated the ceiling above. If prayer "works," it doesn't seem to work very well, or not as often as we would prefer.

Here the wisdom of C. S. Lewis points us in the right direction: "The very question 'Does prayer work?' puts us in the wrong frame of mind from the outset. 'Work': as if it were magic, or a machine—something that functions automatically. Prayer is either a sheer illusion, or else it is a personal contact between embryonic, incomplete persons (ourselves) and the one utterly concrete Person. Prayer in the sense of petition, asking for things, is a small part of it; confession and penitence are its threshold, adoration its sanctuary, the presence and vision and enjoyment of God its bread and wine. In it God shows Himself to us."

Prayer is not something we do because it "works." Think about human relationships. What if I measured my marriage by whether my wife does stuff I want or not? If all I do is come to her with, "Honey, do this, and honey, I want that," you would dismiss me as a stupid husband. A marriage hinges on spending time together, listening, going places, discerning what she might want, loving each other, loving others.

When the great saints of the Church speak of prayer, they very rarely talk about whether it works or not. For them prayer is all about love, the creation of communion with the God from whom the soul cannot bear to be apart. Asking with proper technique is not prayer. As Thérèse of Lisieux wrote about her praying: "I say nothing to him, I love him."

Next we will look more deeply into cultivating such a relationship of love, and how our heartfelt needs and petitions fit into that bigger relationship.

For now, let us pray together: O Lord, without meaning to, I have treated you like a drink machine or a computer search, as if all you want from me is "Gimme, gimme," or

"Help, help," or "I need, I need." What I really need most profoundly, the help I most desperately seek, is an intimate relationship with you. I will persist, I will not be denied. I will take the time to discover you, to be discovered by you, so that we might love each other. O Lord, teach us to pray. *Amen.*

THE WAY TO GOD

He was praying in a certain place, and when he ceased, one of his disciples said to him, "Lord, teach us to pray, as John taught his disciples."
—*Luke 11:1*

So far we have tried to consider how "natural" prayer can be, how we pray as we can, not as we can't, how C. S. Lewis urges us to "lay before Him what is in us, not what ought to be in us." There is no one way to do so, no single formula that applies to everyone. God graces each of us with a peculiar personality.

I went on a prayer retreat a few years ago. We began by taking the Myers-Briggs personality test, and then moved into learning what kind of prayer style is most natural— what fits our personality. My "type" resonates to congregational hymn singing, and to thick books that explore things theological. But a walk in the woods just isn't my thing.

God speaks to each person in a unique way, and each of us speaks to God in a unique way. The better we know ourselves, and how we are wired, the more fruitful our prayer will be. And yet at that retreat we were challenged to grow in our praying. Instead of simply going with what comes easily and naturally, we were instructed to stretch ourselves, to dare to embrace what is difficult, for our goal is to grow as Christians, to discover uncharted terrain with God, to become more like God than we are just at this moment.

The disciples, most of them very devout Jews and fairly well acquainted with Jesus himself, knew they needed to ask, "Lord, teach us to pray." While we all pray in unique ways, we also have much to learn, and there are some common threads in the fabric of every Christian's prayer. The most vital (and beautiful) threads may be utterly unfamiliar to us. No matter who we are, we must learn to pray.

Dietrich Bonhoeffer, as clouds of evil gathered over Europe in 1939, wrote:

"The phrase 'learning to pray' sounds strange to us. If the heart does not overflow and begin to pray by itself, we say, it will never 'learn' to pray. But it is a dangerous error, surely very widespread among Christians, to think that the heart can pray by itself. For then we confuse wishes, hopes, sighs, laments, rejoicings—all of which the heart can do by itself—with prayer.... Prayer does not mean simply to pour out one's heart. It means rather to find the way to God and to speak with him, whether the heart is full or empty."

Prayer is not just "wishing" in front of God. We crave something deeper, and something more consistent. We want a close relationship with God, no matter how our hearts might be feeling at any given moment.

Bonhoeffer used a helpful analogy. Children do not just know how to talk. Rather, "The child learns to speak because his father speaks to him. He learns the speech of his father." So it is as we learn to pray. And the child must be shaped and molded in ways that may not suit the child's immediate desires. "If we are to pray aright, perhaps it is quite necessary that we pray contrary to our own heart. Not what we want to pray is important, but what God wants us to pray. If we were dependent entirely on ourselves, we would probably pray only the fourth petition of the Lord's Prayer. But God wants it otherwise. The richness of the Word of God ought to determine our prayer, not the poverty of our heart."

As God's children, we long for a maturity greater than that fourth petition to "Give us!" Maturity comes from listening to God, by immersing ourselves in God's Word, as we learn a new language, a fascinating new grammar, a kind of talk that begins and ends with no words at all, but sheer silence (to which we turn next).

Let us pray together: Lord, we pray what is in us, but we know this is only the beginning of prayer. Show us the depth, the full essence of your self, the rich mines of life with you. May your Word, not just our words, define our prayer. O Lord, teach us to pray. *Amen.*

SILENCE

For God alone my soul waits in silence.　　　　*—Psalm 62:1*

St. Augustine prayed, "O Lord ... you have made us for yourself, and our heart is restless until it finds rest in you." No index into our restlessness is more telling than our flight from silence. Our world is so noisy, as our planet gets noisier every century. Something is always on, somebody is always saying something. Even our prayers get ruined by a crowd of words.

Why do we fear silence? Perhaps silence feels like loneliness—and we have invested plenty of energy avoiding the truth that we are, in fact, lonely. Even at a party, when we're out in a big gathering, deep inside we may be lonely.

But the paradox is that the antidote to our loneliness isn't more talk, and at the end of the day the ultimate cure to our deepest loneliness isn't any person. No friend, no spouse, nobody can touch the deepest kind of need we have in our hearts. Only God can go there, and be our friend, our fellow, our meaning, our hope.

We are afraid of silence, and so we chase ourselves from one event to another, from one experience to the next, all to avoid looking at ourselves in the mirror. We are afraid of self-discovery, and we are afraid of God—afraid that God might know us, afraid that God just might disturb us, afraid that God might really take us somewhere we prefer not to go.

Do you see? God has made me for God, God has made you for God, and we are wired in such a way that we will forever be miserable until we discover who we are, whose we are—until we are thoroughly known by God, and find ourselves immersed in his love, which casts out all fear.

And we will never know God except by daring to enter into, to stick with, to embrace silence. If we hang with silence in prayer, we discover that we have been foolish to flee our loneliness. What we have needed is solitude, which is the opposite of loneliness. Solitude is when we are alone in the silence, and discover the surprising gift that we are not alone at all. Silence isn't the absence of noise. Rather, silence is a changed way of using our minds. Silence is my soul's availability for God. As Mother Teresa put it, "God is the friend of silence."

So before we pray with words, we are quiet. We wait. Later we speak, but softly, and not too long, waiting in pregnant silence, ending in the quiet stillness. We adapt, and learn to love solitude, which is the startling but steady cure to our loneliness.

Hear Mother Teresa once more: "The beginning of prayer is silence...God speaking in the silence of the heart. And then we start talking to God from the fullness of the heart. And he listens."

And so we pray together, without words, in the quiet. O Lord, teach us to pray. *Amen.*

LESSON ELEVEN

SCRIPTURE

Your word is a lamp to my feet and a light to my path.
—Psalm 119:105 NRSV

D ietrich Bonhoeffer spoke of the child learning to talk
by taking on the language of the parents, and so we
learn to pray by making the Word of God our own.
As Mother Teresa put it, "The beginning of prayer is scripture...we listen to God speaking. And then we begin to
speak to him again from the fullness of our heart. And he
listens. That is really prayer. Both sides listening and both
sides speaking."

We will forever have one-sided conversations in prayer
until we immerse ourselves in Scripture, so both sides listen
and speak. Too much spirituality is free-floating, nothing
more than mental, inner explorations of feelings and
thoughts. Scripture is our anchor, the mooring that keeps us
from drifting into mere wishing, that prevents us from
making prayer self-indulgent.

John Calvin spoke of Scripture as the "mirror" of the
soul. We do not really know ourselves until we look prob-

ingly at ourselves in this mirror of God's Word, which understands the human condition more profoundly than we can ever know ourselves.

Reading the Bible isn't always easy. But remember what Mark Twain said: "It's not the parts of the Bible I don't understand that worry me. It's the parts I *do* understand."

Getting involved with Scripture in prayer is helpful, hopeful, and comforting, but far from easy or comfortable. Reading Scripture is like undergoing surgery, as God uses this "sword of the Spirit" as a scalpel to cut out harmful invaders from our souls. When we use Scripture in prayer, or rather, when we let ourselves be used by Scripture in prayer, we grow, we mature, we extend beyond me and my closed-in interests, and we begin to share in the mind of God, "both sides listening and both sides speaking."

The parts of the Bible that may actually be easiest for us to understand, no matter our background, no matter our lack of Bible knowledge, are the Psalms. The four Gospels are also especially fruitful in terms of prayer, and we will consider how to use these portions of Scripture in Lesson 12.

And so we pray together: O Lord, I do not yet know your language, your grammar. Help me to read, to become familiar with your words, your stories, the path you would set me on. Jerk me out of my narrow interests in prayer and into the way you look at the whole universe. I want your Son, Jesus, to be on my mind. O Lord, teach us to pray. *Amen.*

JESUS PRAYED THE PSALMS

My God, my God, why have you forsaken me?   —*Psalm 22:1 NRSV*

I f prayer begins with Scripture, we are wisest to begin with the Psalms. Anybody can read a Psalm and make sense of it. Most Psalms are short, and easy to identify with. The Psalms are simply prayers, and they express in profound ways our relationship to God. The Psalms teach us to pray. Christoph Barth called the Psalms a school of prayer.

How easy is it to enter into a Psalm and pray, to make its words your prayer? Psalm 130 begins, "Out of the depths I cry to you, O LORD" (NRSV). What depths do you know? And what depths are you in? Psalm 69 begins, "Save me, O God! For the waters have come up to my neck." This person isn't literally drowning—but you may be drowning in something you've had "up to here!" Jesus, on the Cross, prayed a Psalm, the twenty-second: "My God, my God, why have you forsaken me?" Ever felt forsaken by God? The Psalms are brutally honest, and they can help us know ourselves honestly, and to pray honestly before God.

And yet the Psalms, and the rest of the Bible, stretch us beyond the kind of praying that forever gets sucked into "me and my concerns." The Bible lures us out of our small world and into God's huge world. We begin to know God's worries, to feel God's pain for people beyond our small circle.

A simple habit, practiced by millions of Christians for centuries, is to pray one Psalm per day, or one in the morning and another in the evening, just working your way through. I did this when I was in seminary—and I did it in a hospital room with a young friend who was dying. Powerful, poignant prayers...and my friend Thaniel over several weeks was ushered by beautiful Psalms through a horrific struggle with cystic fibrosis into the arms of her Lord.

All of the Bible can be prayed. St. Ignatius recommended a kind of visual prayer, where we enter into any Bible story and make it a prayer. We hear about Jesus on the road, and a blind man cries out. We imagine the dirt, the dust, the noise from the city, the face of the blind man. We ask who is crying out for help in our world. We contemplate our own blindness. We close our eyes and imagine our cry to Jesus, and hear his voice. We open our eyes, and we see the world anew.

We hear about Jesus and some fishermen. We imagine the waves lapping against the boat, the smell of fish and sweat. We imagine the surprise of Jesus speaking. It is to us he says, "Put down your nets and follow me." What net is in my hand? What do I need to lay down to follow him?

The Crucifixion is a particularly poignant moment for prayer. We read about Jesus' suffering, and in prayer we feel his pain, measure his grief. We converse with Jesus, as if we were standing at the foot of the cross. Why are you enduring this? For me? For my family? For my friend? For my enemy?

St. Francis, contemplating the Crucifixion, prayed: "O Lord, two graces I ask of you before I die: first, that I may feel in my soul and body that anguish you underwent in the hour of your passion. And second, that I may feel in my soul and body the love you felt so as willingly to undergo such suffering for us sinners."

Prayer, when all is said and done, may be nothing more than thinking about Jesus, being in constant relationship with Jesus. I love what Dorothy Day said near the end of her life. She was going to write a summary of what mattered most in her life, but she couldn't. "I just sat there and thought of our Lord, and His visit to us all those centuries ago, and I said to myself that my great luck was to have had Him on my mind for so long in my life!"

And so let us pray together: O Lord, thank you for Scripture, your fascinating, precious gift of words to us. Help us to see our true selves, and your glory, in the mirror of your Word. O Lord, teach us to pray. *Amen.*

WORSHIP

And they devoted themselves to the apostles' teaching and fellowship, to the breaking of bread and the prayers. —*Acts 2:42*

A nnie Dillard tells about a church she attended near Puget Sound. The minister was kneeling at the altar one week, leading the congregation in prayer. Suddenly he stopped, looked up toward the ceiling, and cried out, "Lord, we bring you these same petitions every week." Then the service proceeded. Dillard wrote, "Because of this, I like him very much."

Perhaps the most crucial school of prayer is our weekly worship. We say the same prayers every week. Søren Kierkegaard helped us understand worship: while a service looks like performers (the minister, the choir) on stage before an audience (the congregation), the fact is that we all are the performers (minister, choir, congregation), and God is the audience. All worship is a prayer made profound and meaningful because we do it with others. We are not alone.

In worship we declare what is worthy of our praise, another countercultural act in a world where everything from soap to cars is praised. In worship we offer ourselves and what we have to God. In worship we are even transformed into people we would never be had we not come.

We are stretched to pray together what we probably would not pray alone. The Church bears this weighty burden in worship to talk of life and death, to remind people of what they would prefer to forget. The Church in worship calls us out of our narrow world of self-interest and forces us to pray for people we do not know or have never seen. The Church in worship speaks of evil, sin—unpleasant subjects, yet essential to the fullness of life with God.

Hymns teach us to pray. Martin Luther used pointed words to praise hymn singing:

"Music is a fair and lovely gift of God which has often wakened and moved me to . . . joy. . . . I have no use for cranks who despise music, because it is a gift of God. Music drives away the Devil and makes people gay; they forget thereby all wrath, unchastity, arrogance, and the like. . . . This precious gift has been bestowed on men . . . to remind them that they are created to praise and magnify the Lord. But when natural music is sharpened and polished by art, then one begins to see with amazement the great and perfect wisdom of God in his wonderful work of music, where one voice takes a simple part and around it sing three, four, or five other voices, leaping, springing round about, marvelously gracing the simple part, like a square dance in heaven with friendly bows, embracings, and hearty swinging of the partners. He who does not find this an inexpressible miracle of the Lord is truly a clod."

We are clods if we want a solo relationship with God. We were made to pray together. Community prayer is the norm, the basis, for all our private prayers, not vice versa.

All acts of worship are prayers. St. Augustine said baptism is a "visible prayer," as in every baptism we do not marvel at how cute the baby is, but we marvel that God loves all of us as children; not only do these parents or the one being baptized offer themselves to God, but we too offer our lives up to God once more. Catholics, on entering a church, will dip a finger into the baptismal font, touch the water to the forehead, and say, "I am baptized"—and Luther argued there can be no greater comfort in this life. Similarly with the Lord's Supper, we give thanks to God, remember in prayer our salvation, and devour a tangible reminder of the Crucifixion of our Lord.

And so let us pray together: O Lord, we say the same prayers every week, together. Thank you for our life of worship. Forgive us for watching it, like a show. Help us to enter into our common worship, to discover that when we gather together, you are most profoundly there. May we be buoyed by the truth that your community goes with us into all our private places and solitary prayers, so that we truly are never alone. O Lord, teach us to pray. *Amen.*

SAINTS

Therefore, since we are surrounded by so great a cloud of witnesses, let us also lay aside every weight, and sin which clings so closely, and let us run with perseverance the race that is set before us, looking to Jesus the pioneer and perfecter of our faith.   *—Hebrews 12:1-2*

We learn to pray in worship with others. But the miracle of Christian community is even more astonishing than we can fathom. The extraordinary privilege of the Church is that we live among saints, visible and invisible. We dwell, even today, among heroes who lived centuries ago, who lived on the other side of the world. We are not the first people to pray, to struggle, to break through, to wonder. A great cloud of saints, some famous and well known throughout the Church, others no better known than your grandmother, pray with us as we pray. When we praise God, they join in the chorus. When we cry out in need, they intercede for us.

Just as an apprentice learns a trade from a master craftsman, so we learn prayer from saints who have known God better than we do. We remember how they prayed, the way they prayed. This will require some remembering. I remember my grandfather, Papa Howell, well. I don't remember him telling me, "James, you'd better pray." But I do remember stumbling into his room unannounced, only to find him on his knees with his Bible open, his prayer interrupted, his example forever etched in my soul.

To learn from the masters may require some effort, some research. I wrote a book a couple of years ago on the saints, and I devoted a whole chapter to saints who were stalwarts in prayer. St. Francis knew God intimately. Legend has it that St. Teresa of Avila had to cling to the altar rail during prayer to keep from floating upward! But at the heart of her relationship with God were two impulses without which we will never be close to God: discipline, the regular practice of prayer, and an opening up of the emotional life to God. What we bring to God is not great holiness and wisdom (even if you are a saint), but brokenness and profound need, a virtually desperate desire to be loved, held, and swept up into the very heart of God. Our weakness is not something to be corrected, but becomes the very crucible in which intimacy with God is established.

In the late nineteenth century, Thérèse of Lisieux could speak almost romantically of her prayer life. She imagined a kiss from Jesus, a deep sense of love. Above the doorway to her room she carved, "Jesus is my only love." She wrote poetry expressing her passion to be on fire with love for Jesus, her craving to be with Jesus forever.

Learn about a saint or two. Purchase an icon, or a painting or photo of a spiritual hero, hang it on your wall. Let their lives, their example, inspire you.

With great profit, we may simply pray the prayers of the saints. I'll use as our closing prayer some words I love from the Middle Ages by Thomas à Kempis.

Let us pray together: Lord, in what can I trust in this life? And what is my greatest comfort on earth? Is it not

Yourself, O Lord my God, whose mercy is limitless? Have I ever prospered without You? And did I ever suffer ill when You were at hand? I would rather be poor for Your sake than rich without You. I would choose to be a wanderer on the face of the earth with You, rather than to possess heaven without You. For where You are, there is Heaven; and where You are not, there is death and Hell. You are my sole desire; for You I sigh, pray, and cry. . . . Unless You abide with me, all things that seem to bring peace and happiness are as nothing, for they cannot bestow true happiness. You alone are the End of all good things, the fullness of life, the depth of wisdom; and the greatest comfort of Your servants is to trust in You above all else. My God, Father of mercies, I look to You, I trust in You.

Amen.

FASTING

And when you fast, do not look dismal, like the hypocrites. . . . But when you fast, anoint your head and wash your face . . . and your Father who sees in secret will reward you.   —*Matthew 6:16-18*

B efore we turn to the subjects of prayer, the content of our time with God (praise, giving thanks, confession, intercession, meditation), I want to reiterate a few practical matters. Remember the importance of place and atmosphere. Find a place to set aside, some sanctified spot for your praying, and you may need to furnish it however simply with a photo, an icon of a saint, a candle, a memento, something to draw you into the mood of prayer. Don't forget that a crucifix or picture of some saint hanging in your hallway might be a regular reminder as you move from room to room that, yes, there is a God, that yes, Jesus died for me, that yes, my purpose on this planet is to live for God.

Pay attention to your body and its rhythms. The saints remind us that we pray most poorly when we are "full"— when we're rushing here and there, and perhaps especially after a big meal. Interestingly, the most productive way to grow in prayer might be something so simple as not eating or drinking so much, even skipping a meal or two.

John Wesley prescribed several disciplines that he called "means of grace": prayer, Bible reading, and fasting are among them. Nothing is more alien to our culture than fasting. But consider Moses, Elijah, David, Paul, Jesus himself, Augustine, Francis, Luther, Calvin, Teresa: all knew that renunciation is the only route to fulfillment. This is especially important in our consumer culture that says I must satisfy every animal craving, that being filled equals the good life.

Fasting is not giving up something harmful, like smoking or double martinis. Fasting is giving up something good in itself, something I have and love, but which I do without for a time for the sake of God. When we satisfy every desire, and as often as possible, then our deeper desire for God comes to be masked over, desensitized. I need to fast as a reminder that I have a deeper quest than the satisfaction of my animal desires. I blunt those desires to whet my appetite for God. When hunger gnaws, I discover how hollow I am inside, how superficial I can be. Richard J. Foster, in his helpful book on spiritual disciplines, says, "Our human cravings and desires are like rivers that tend to overflow their banks; fasting helps keep them in their proper channels."

We also learn a solidarity with the needy, who by no choice of their own are denied simple pleasures and satisfactions. There is the danger of self-pity and self-righteousness in fasting. Francis of Assisi once fasted for forty days, but on the thirty-ninth day he broke the fast, eating half a loaf of bread—in order to avoid vainglory, as he might be tempted to think he was as holy as Jesus. Doing without the basics, and even shedding a luxury or two, should lead to simplicity, as the Christian life knows the freedom of which the Shakers sing: "'Tis a gift to be simple, 'tis a gift to be free." Every day we have thousands of choices, and if over and over we choose the simpler way, if in various ways we choose renunciation, then we are less and less enmeshed in the world, and have more freedom, an available space for God.

Right now we might consider that in times of national crisis, the people of Israel all fasted, prayed together, denied themselves together, seeking relief and hope from God.

And so let us pray together: O Lord, we are so full of so much. And yet we feel empty. Clearly the reason must be that we aren't really empty, but rather we are full of the wrong stuff. We would be filled with you, and so we dare to make room for you, by fasting from indulging so much, by voluntarily going hungry, for you alone can satisfy us, as individuals, and as a people. O Lord, teach us to pray. *Amen.*

A COPERNICAN REVOLUTION

O LORD, our Lord, how majestic is your name in all the earth...whose glory above the heavens is chanted.   —*Psalm 8:1 A.P.*

Thus far we have considered the importance of prayer, our need to pray, obstacles to doing so, and some practicalities of prayer. Now we turn to the subjects, the themes, the content of prayer.

The ultimate point of prayer is, of course, God, and as we grow in prayer we grow toward God. More and more of our attention is riveted upon God. Listen to Richard Foster:

"In the beginning we are indeed the subject and the center of our prayers. But in God's time and in God's way a Copernican revolution takes place in our heart. Slowly, almost imperceptibly, there is a shift in our center of gravity. We pass from thinking of God as part of our life to the realization that we are part of his life. Wondrously and mysteriously God moves from the periphery of our prayer experience to the center."

This revolution echoes something Dietrich Bonhoeffer wrote from his cell in a Nazi concentration camp. He said that our life with God "is not in the first place thinking about one's own needs, problems, sins, and fears, but allowing oneself to be caught up into the way of Jesus Christ." The paradox, of course, is that the more I am caught up into the way of Jesus Christ, the more I am swept up into a relationship of love with my Maker, the more my needs, problems, sins, and fears come to be healed, understood, and even utilized for the good.

From one perspective, a heroic, gargantuan effort is required for us to break out of our self-absorbed shell so that our prayers might be about God. With practice we most certainly can grow in thinking of our lives as part of God's life, in letting God occupy the center of our thoughts.

But even the most titanic effort will fail, partly because we are human, and we are sinful. The best we can muster is to *want* God at the center. But our desire to have God at the heart of life is pleasing to God. The real revolution in our prayer life comes when we realize we are not capable of thinking or even praying as we ought. But Christ is able, and if we are open and on the lookout for it, the Holy Spirit will grace us with a gift, with a middling but definite realization that God *is* the center, whether we've placed God there or not. And this recognition is liberating—a divine relief—humbling but hopeful.

This knowledge may lead us to cope with frustration in prayer. Maggie Ross suggested:

"We are outraged when God does not seem to respond to *our* prayer, when God does not seem to make things go according to *our* plan. It rarely occurs to us that in this seeming refusal God is perhaps leading us, offering us greater possibility, giving us the opportunity to be led into a wider place...out of bondage from our tunnel vision, and into a larger life and freedom."

Praying, focusing on God, being caught up in the divine adventure, is our freedom. So our closing prayer will be one conceived by St. Francis of Assisi, a prayer that can nudge the center of gravity in our souls toward our Lord.

Let us pray together:

You are the holy Lord God . . .
You are good, all good, the highest good,
Lord God living and true.

You are love, charity; You are wisdom, You are humility,
You are patience, You are beauty, You are meekness,
You are security, You are rest,
You are gladness and joy, You are our hope, You are justice,
You are moderation, You are all our riches to sufficiency.

You are beauty, You are meekness,
You are the protector, You are our custodian and defender,
You are strength, You are refreshment, You are our hope,
You are our faith, You are our charity,
You are all our sweetness, You are our eternal life:
Great and wonderful Lord, Almighy God,
    Merciful Savior.

O Lord, teach us to pray. *Amen.*

PRAISE

Great is the LORD, and greatly to be praised. —*Psalm 145:3*

The first reflex in prayer is praise. God is great, awesome, loving, beautiful—the list can and must go on and on. Praise is cheap nowadays. In advertising, everything gets praised, from cars to hairspray, from burgers to lawnmowers. But the only ultimately praiseworthy object of our adoration is God, the creator of it all, the giver of all good.

St. Augustine made an important distinction between two Latin words used in his day for love. First there is *uti* love, love of "use." I may love money, not because I delight in handling it or hanging it framed on my wall. I only love money because I can use it for something else. Then there is *frui* love, love of "enjoyment." I love chocolate, not because of what I use it for (which isn't all that advantageous to my waistline or cholesterol level). I just love it, will go to great lengths to get it. Augustine suggested that too often we love God with *uti* love: we want to use God to get other things we really want. What God yearns for from us is *frui* love, when we simply love God because of who God is, what God has done, no matter what we get out of it, no matter what that love might cost us.

Praise is our amazement at God and God's goodness, our recognition of the power and tenderness of the creator. Praise is enjoying and celebrating God's love. Praise is our best attempt to feel, say, or sing something appropriate to God.

Praise is what we were made for. And yet in our busy lives, praise of God will require some time, even some training. Praise doesn't "work," it is not productive, it isn't even about me. Praise means being lost in adoration of the beloved, being awestruck by beauty. Praise is downright wasteful in terms of possible ways to spend your time. To think of God like a lover, one on whom you might dote for hours, requires considerable imagination, a radical reshaping of the soul.

To learn praise we need a guide, someone like St. Francis, who wrote his famous canticle: "Most High, all-powerful, good Lord, Yours are *the praises,* the glory, and *the honor,* and the *blessing,* to You alone, Most High, do they belong, and no human is worthy to mention Your name. Praised be You, my *Lord,* with all *Your creatures.*" He proceeds to praise God for "Sir Brother Sun, who is the day... and bears a likeness of You, Most High One"; then he turns to Sister Moon and the stars, Brother Wind, Sister Water, Brother Fire, and Sister Mother Earth. Poignantly, Francis composed these lyrics not long before his death, while racked with pain, suffering constant hemorrhaging, his eyesight almost gone. Francis and other saints have taught us a paradox in praise, how the very effort to praise God is an antidote to despair.

On his deathbed in 1791, with a handful of friends gathered to wait and watch, John Wesley surprised everyone when he broke a long silence by breaking into song (from a hymn by Isaac Watts): "I'll praise my Maker while I've breath; and when my voice is lost in death, praise shall employ my nobler powers. My days of praise shall ne'er be past. . . ." Had we been able to ask Wesley what he would be doing two or three hundred years after his death, he would confidently have answered with those same words.

Of course, no better primer in praise could exist than the Psalms. Let us read, pray, and praise Psalms, especially Psalms 8, 19, 33, 96, 103, 139, 145.

Let us pray together the shortest Psalm, 117: Praise the LORD, all nations! Extol him, all peoples! For great is his steadfast love toward us; and the faithfulness of the LORD endures forever. Praise the LORD! *Amen.*

GRATITUDE

O give thanks to the LORD, for he is good. —Psalm 106:1

From our first theme in prayer, praise, we move toward a related mood: giving thanks. Praise is being awestruck and glorifying God for who God is. Thanks is being dumbfounded and grateful for what God has done for us.

The ancient Israelites enjoyed a huge advantage over us in terms of feeling grateful. Lacking technology and financial security, they knew they were utterly dependent upon God for their bread (if they had any bread), for shelter (if they had any shelter), for taking that next breath, for the sunshine and rain. We modern people are so smart, so self-sufficient—and especially in America, where we prize independence above all else.

We think of gratitude as a feeling that you either have spontaneously, or you just don't have—and generally we don't. We nurture grievances and file complaints. Advertisers incessantly lull us into a sense of dissatisfaction, so we will buy their products. Even the season of Thanksgiving becomes one more day of vacation, when the malls have sales and we gorge ourselves with a bit too much turkey and dressing.

Perhaps our hardest lesson in prayer is to develop this counterintuitive sense of dependence. I am not the master of my fate. It's not all up to me. I don't "earn" what is genuinely good in life. It is all gift, all grace.

Henri Nouwen understood how gratitude takes practice:

"The discipline of gratitude is the explicit effort to acknowledge that all I am and have is given to me as a gift of love, a gift to be celebrated with joy.

"Gratitude as a discipline involves a conscious choice. I can choose to be grateful even when my emotions and feelings are still steeped in hurt and resentment. It is amazing how many occasions present themselves in which I can choose gratitude instead of a complaint. I can choose to be grateful when I am criticized, even when my heart still responds in bitterness. I can choose to speak about goodness and beauty, even when my inner eye looks for someone to accuse or something to call ugly. I can choose to listen to the voices that forgive and to look at the faces that smile, even while I still hear words of revenge and grimaces of hatred....

"The choice for gratitude rarely comes without some real effort. But each time I make it, the next choice is a little easier, a little freer, a little less self-conscious.... Acts of gratitude make one grateful."

The Psalms, once again, are a mighty chorus of thanks to God. In fact, many of the Psalms (such as 30, 34, 66, 126) were little worship services in which you would gather with family, neighbors, and friends, and tell the story of "what God has done for me." As a tangible expression of your gratitude, you would give an offering—your best sheep, the first wheat that ripened—as thanks to God. To grow in gratitude, we will probably need to be sure our gratitude is tangible, involving our stuff, offered to God, shared with the poor. And we will need to learn how to tell our story—to someone unsure about God, to someone who may be losing hope, to someone who's burdened by "earning" and toting the weight of the world on his or her shoulders.

So let us pray together, using Psalm 118:21-28 (NRSV): I thank you that you have answered me and become my salvation. You are my God, and I will give thanks to you. This is the day the LORD has made; let us rejoice and be glad in it. *Amen.*

CONFESSION

If we say we have no sin, we deceive ourselves.... If we confess our sins, he is faithful and just, and will forgive our sins and cleanse us from all unrighteousness. —1 John 1:8-9

The most unpleasant theme of prayer we would prefer to forget is the embarrassment of sin. Modern, secular society discounts the very notion of sin. Thoughts and behaviors long bracketed under the category of "sin" now are "explained" in psychological categories. Or we blithely conclude, "Hey, I'm a pretty good person," figuring that, if God grades on the curve, we'll pass. Worst of all, we tragically glamorize sin. For centuries, the Church has taught that there are seven deadly sins: pride, greed, lust, sloth, gluttony, anger, envy. But these sound like the good life! Why shouldn't God loosen up and let us enjoy living?

This is important: prayer isn't when we grit our teeth and embrace an unpleasant life. Instead, prayer is when we discover what a truly pleasant life is—and true happiness is not won through addictions to greed, lust, sloth, and envy. Through the eyes of faith we see that sin is the most self-destructive thing imaginable. There is a deeper kind of self-ishness that says "The absolute best thing I can do for myself, and for others, is to praise and serve God."

C. S. Lewis hazarded the guess that nowadays, good people regard "unselfishness" as the highest virtue, whereas the great Christians of old would have thought of "love." We have substituted a negative, assuming somehow that desires should be denied, smothered, cooled. Then he adds:

"Indeed, if we consider the unblushing promises of reward and the staggering nature of the rewards promised in the Gospels, it would seem that Our Lord finds our desires not too strong, but too weak. We are half-hearted creatures, fooling about with drink and sex and ambition when infinite joy is offered us, like an ignorant child who wants to go on making mud pies in a slum because he cannot imagine what is meant by the offer of a holiday at the sea. We are far too easily pleased."

We sin. Martin Luther spoke of sin as being "curved in" on your self. Sin indeed is living as if I am the center of the universe, as if everything exists for me. Like Narcissus, I gaze on my reflection and fall in love. Like Atlas, I bear the weight of the world on my shoulders.

But I am not good at being God, and you aren't either. Sensing this, at times we veer off and fawn after other gods, who aren't God either. Martin Luther King Jr. painted the disaster involved:

"There is so much frustration in the world because we have relied on gods rather than God. We have genuflected before the god of science only to find that it has given us the atomic bomb. . . . We have worshipped the god of pleasure only to discover that thrills play out and sensations are short-lived. We have bowed before the god of money only to learn that there are such things as love and friendship that money cannot buy. . . . These transitory gods are not able to save or bring happiness to the human heart. Only God is able."

Prayer will forever be frustrated until we recognize there is a massive gulf between us and God—and God didn't put it there. We sin, we keep God at arm's distance, we amass a cloud of selfishness and lack of love and bogus gods in the space where we should rest in God's love.

In the next several lessons, I will say more about sin, repentance, and forgiveness.

For now, let us pray together: O Lord, we have lost our sense of sin. We are experts at justifying our existence. I want to believe I am okay the way I am. Lord, create in my soul an awareness of my sin, of how I wound you by my coldness, of how I get out of sync with your intentions for me, how I have so many thoughts and motives that are not of you. I have genuflected before other gods who cannot deliver. Remind me that you desire only the best for me, not a life of misery, but a life of joy and purpose. Help me to face the unpleasant facts about myself. Strengthen my desires. O Lord, teach us to pray. *Amen.*

NOT YOUR FAULT

O LORD, you have brought up my soul from the pit.—Psalm 30:3 A.T.

To speak of confession, we need to make a few seemingly subtle but huge distinctions. Confession is about sin and guilt, and guilt is very different from shame. Guilt may be my very real sense of remorse over ways I have faltered. But shame involves not bad things I have done, but bad things that have been done to me.

Confession isn't plunging into a dark mood of self-recrimination. We may bear a brutal weight of negative views of our selves. There are always people who will dump garbage into our souls. But low self-esteem isn't the same as discovering you have sinned. Huddling beneath humiliation because you have been abused does not make you somehow unworthy in God's eyes. Shame requires much prayer—but a different kind of praying, a prayer for healing, for forgiveness and more.

I love the poignant scene in the film *Good Will Hunting*, when this therapist, Sean McGuire (played by Robin Williams), after many weeks of therapy with Will Hunting (played by Matt Damon), learns that the young man's aberrant behaviors stem from pretty severe childhood abuse. He embraces the tough Will and keeps repeating, "It's not your fault, it's not your fault, it's not your fault," and finally Will breaks down and sobs.

As we grapple seriously with sin, and our very real rebellion against God, we need to recognize that God isn't a harsh taskmaster, flinging blame everywhere. God will embrace us and understand much that plagues us and insist that "It's not your fault," and bring healing.

The confession of sin isn't about groveling and feeling really yucky about yourself. God has no interest in scenarios in which we look in the mirror, notice our waywardness, and then bemoan how lousy we've been. Confession is about healing a relationship. Confession is about change. Getting mired in morose feelings and guilt is not God's plan for us. God is luring us toward joy, fulfillment, a new life.

Confession at the end of the day isn't about feelings at all. Jesus came, not so we might feel different, but so we might be different. To be different, we must recognize a disability on our part. We cannot simply grit our teeth and "Just say no," or just start being holy. My determination to do better, on its own, will flounder in the most embarrassing ways. The most futile wild goose chase is the avoidance of sin. On our own we cannot be good. Goodness is a gift from God, something we discover, a power working through and in spite of ourselves. At the heart of things, confession is about love. For the antithesis of sin is not goodness, but love.

And love is all gift. Remember how Frederick Buechner described our plight and our hope: we live our lives like a big clenched fist, which can work and fight—but that clenched fist can never accept a helping hand. That clenched fist also clings to guilt and poisons that God would take from us, if only we relax, and trust God with open hands.

And so let us pray together: O Lord, my life is a clenched fist. I am hanging on to so much—mostly to my determination to make it on my own. Help me. Take me by the hand. Reach into my soul and help me discern where I am a sinner, turned against you, and where I have been sinned against, and in need of your healing touch. Make us different. O Lord, teach us to pray. *Amen.*

REPENTANCE

Jesus came into Galilee, preaching the gospel of God, and saying... "The kingdom of God is at hand; repent, and believe in the gospel."
—Mark 1:14-15

John Wesley talked about the religious life as entering a home. The porch is repentance, the door is faith, and holiness is life inside the home. But what does it mean to repent?

The Hebrew word in the Old Testament translated "repent" is *shûb* (pronounced 'shoov'), which means to make a 180-degree turn. You are going in the wrong direction! To repent means to turn around, to quit running from God, and turn back toward God.

The Greek word in the New Testament translated "repent" is *metanoia*, which means "a change of mind." Repentance isn't groveling and feeling bad. To repent is to get reoriented, to move in a new direction, to look at the world from God's perspective, to take on the mind of Christ.

So to repent is not merely to apologize, or to admit wrongdoing, like George Washington: "I cannot tell a lie, I did chop down the cherry tree." Repentance is all about healing and change.

The beginning of repentance is when we dare to know what God wants from us, and to take that claim with total seriousness. We learn God's ways through understanding the Bible, through prayer, through conversation with wise Christians.

The work of repentance is never done. Catherine of Siena prayed, "You, eternal Trinity, are a deep sea: The more I enter you, the more I discover, and the more I discover, the more I seek you"—and the more we discover that we are not yet of God. We pray, we confess, we change—and then we discover not that we are now holy, but rather we realize that even in our improved state we are not yet fully in God's hands. There is forever some unhanded-over knot in the soul, some unexamined corner of the psyche, some carefully sheltered behavior we have not yet yielded to God.

We forever need forgiveness. We never master the Christian life. Our minds are never pure. But this discovery need not depress us. Instead, this is our hope. Otherwise we are stuck in a rut of our own burrowing, when God is reaching down to lift us up into newness of life.

At the beginning of the day, we pray for God to keep us out of sin, to create in us the recognition of dangers, to nudge us toward holiness. And at the end of every day, we are wise to take stock in the day, to note with brutal honesty and frankness where we have veered from God's way, how we have been careless with the opportunities God has given us, how we have been ungrateful, unkind, downright ugly, apathetic, critical of others.

And so we pray together, using the words Thomas Cranmer wrote more than four hundred years ago for the *Book of Common Prayer*:

"Almighty and most merciful Father; we have erred, and strayed from thy ways like lost sheep. We have followed too much the devices and desires of our own hearts. We have offended against thy holy laws. We have left undone those things which we ought to have done; and we have done those things which we ought not to have done; and there is no health in us. But thou, O Lord, have mercy upon us, miserable offenders. Spare those, O God, who confess their faults. Restore those who are penitent, according to thy promises declared unto mankind in Christ Jesus our Lord. And grant, O most merciful Father, for his sake, that we may hereafter live a godly, righteous, and sober life, to the glory of thy holy Name. Amen."

FORGIVENESS (PART 1)

Forgive us our trespasses, as we forgive those who trespass against us.
—*Luke 11:2*

There is a great scene in John Irving's *The World According to Garp*. Garp and his wife, Helen, have hurt each other in unspeakable ways. Garp breaks the long, angry silence by scribbling a note to Helen: "I don't blame you." After a while, he writes another: "I don't blame *me*, either." Then a third note follows: "Only in this way can we be whole again."

Prayer is drawn toward forgiveness, God forgiving us, our forgiving each other, an end to all blaming, for only in this way can we be whole again.

When Jesus taught the disciples to pray, he grabbed hold of vertical forgiveness, "O Lord, forgive me, for I have sinned," and nailed it to horizontal forgiveness, "...as we forgive those who trespass against us," two interrelated acts of forgiveness, forming a cross. Jesus not only taught about forgiveness. He became forgiveness. He makes forgiveness possible and real.

Catherine of Siena described the wood of the cross as forming a bridge, one that crosses that chasm—that gulf—between our wayward lives and a loving God. In prayer we walk across that bridge, feel it firmly beneath our feet, and manage to find our way home to God. "The LORD is merciful . . . He will not always chide, nor will he keep his anger for ever. He does not deal with us according to our sins, nor requite us according to our iniquities. . . . As a father pities his children, so the Lord pities those who fear him. For he knows our frame; he remembers that we are dust" (Psalm 103:8-10, 13-14).

We pray for forgiveness, and trust that it is given—but not lightly! Forgiveness is costly—to God, and to us. To God, in that he bears our lack of love, our rebellion. His son bore all our recalcitrance on his heart, which was shattered by the weight of our sin. But it is all borne, and not by us, but by God. Realizing the cost to God is painfully grievous to us. When we recognize the depth of God's love and sacrifice for us, it costs us our lives. But therein we find our life, our love, and our hope.

Living a forgiven life is more than simply relief that we have been absolved. Forgiveness is living with the abiding sense of what our relationship with God and other people can be, and so forgiveness motivates us, admonishes us, provokes us to enrich our poor relationships. Or as Abraham Lincoln put it to a startled questioner near the end of the Civil War: "Madam, do I not destroy my enemies when I make them my friends?" God has destroyed us as enemies, and made us friends, which pivots us outward to destroy our own enemies by making them our friends. Prayer is friendship.

And so we pray together: O Lord, forgive us of our sins. Make us aware of them, and inspire us to offer them up as a sacrifice on the fire of your love. Destroy whatever is out of sync with you that is in us, and befriend us. Show us what it is like to be whole again, and in reconciled peace with you and each other. O Lord, teach us to pray. *Amen.*

FORGIVENESS (PART 2)

Be angry but do not sin; do not let the sun go down on your anger. . . .
Let all bitterness and wrath and anger . . . be put away from you . . .
be kind to one another, tenderhearted, forgiving one another, as God in
Christ forgave you. —*Ephesians 4:26, 31-32*

Forgiveness, to give it, or to receive it, involves a loss of control. We live in a world that craves control, so we resort to blaming, to punishing, to winners and losers. But forgiveness casts out all blaming, all winning and losing. Forgiveness brings peace.

Frederick Buechner wrote, "When somebody you've wronged forgives you, you're spared the dull throb of a guilty conscience. When you forgive somebody who has wronged you, you're spared the dismal corrosion of bitterness and wounded pride. For both parties, forgiveness means the freedom again to be at peace inside their own skins and to be glad in each other's presence."

At times we discover miraculous reconciliation, miraculous in the sense that we are never fully capable of forgiveness. Forgiveness isn't saying, "It doesn't matter." It matters

—but we can reconcile anyhow. That's why in Bible times they performed all those smelly-sounding sacrifices with the blood of oxen and lambs. It is as if, when we have hurt each other, some residue of guilt lingers between us. No matter what we do to patch things up, some gap remains that we cannot cross. They shed the animal's blood, believing that God's healing power was released. And so we need the healing power of God's forgiveness, in the sacrifice of Christ, to bridge those residual gaps between each other, and between us and God. Prayer voices our need for a power beyond our capability.

Forgiveness requires work. Forgiveness is something we practice, taking the trouble to be in the presence of another person, daring to tell the truth in love, seeing deeply enough to understand the profound and painful causes of what has gone on between us and the other person, even confessing our own complicity. Jesus hilariously reminded us how good we are at spotting specks in other people's eyes while totally missing a log in our own (Matthew 7:1-5). We work, knowing we will fail, daring to succeed, always remembering God's mercy for us is beyond anything we could ever extend to another person. Prayers for forgiveness commit us to get busy.

Sometimes forgiveness happens in our imaginations (but is no less marvelous for it)! The Greek word frequently translated "forgive" is *aphiemi*, a word that means to drop, to open your hand and just let whatever is in it fall to the ground. Forgiveness is not about warm fuzzy feelings. Sometimes we feel we cannot forgive someone who has been brutal to us, someone who stole our childhood, or hurt our child. But forgiveness isn't always about warm feelings. Forgiveness can be simply letting go, refusing to continue to nurture some grievance, for as we cradle a wrong near our hearts, we continue to corrode our own hearts. We let go. By God's power, we forgive. We move on. We pray, and feel God pat our fists that cling so tightly, to relax, to let go, to forgive.

In memory, in tangible reality, and in hope, we pray for forgiveness, and discover ourselves grasped gently but firmly by the love of Christ. Martin Luther King Jr. was right: "Love is the only force capable of transforming an enemy into a friend. We never get rid of an enemy by meeting hate with hate. We get rid of an enemy by getting rid of enmity. By its very nature, hate destroys and tears down. But love creates and builds up. Love transforms with redemptive power."

And so we pray together: O Lord, we need forgiveness—in our souls, and between me and someone I'd prefer to avoid. Or between me and someone I cannot even talk to any longer. Between me and someone in my family, a friend, a neighbor, some child of yours. Grant us the miracle of forgiveness, of reconciliation, or of letting go. O Lord, teach us to pray. *Amen.*

WOUNDS

Be gracious to me, O LORD, for I am languishing. . . . My soul also is sorely troubled. . . . O LORD—how long?   —*Psalm 6:2-3*

We don't need a tutor in prayer to help us recognize that the philosopher Hobbes was right: life is "solitary, poor, nasty, brutish, and short." We all have wounds, terrible burdens, agonizing situations. Some blindside us unexpectedly in the dark. Others are grinding, nagging at us over seemingly endless years.

The lesson of prayer is that we are not in fact "solitary." Normally we bear our sufferings alone. Or we hope a friend, a lover, or some professional will help, will heal, will fill the void, ease the pain. And they may—but only in part. For there is a place deep within every soul, the place that really hurts, the place in us that weeps—and no person, no matter how loving or noble, can go there. Only Christ can go that deep into the marrow of our soul.

Henri Nouwen, imagining himself talking with Christ hanging on the cross, prayed:

"O Lord, why is it that I am so eager to receive human praise and human support even when experience tells me how limited and conditional is the love that comes from a human heart? So many have shown me their love...but no one could touch that deep, hidden place where my fear and my loneliness dwell. Only you know that place, Lord... How can I ever go anywhere else but to you to find the love I so desire! How can I expect from people as sinful as myself a love that can touch the most hidden corners of my being? Who can wash me clean as you do and give me food and drink as you do? Who wants me to be so close, so intimate and so safe as you do?"

Dietrich Bonhoeffer recommended we turn to the Psalms, so many of which cry out to God for some relief, for some comfort, for any slight sign of hope. As we pray the Psalms, we discover that they "cast every difficulty and agony on God: 'We can no longer bear it, take it from us and bear it yourself, you alone can handle suffering.'"

For the message of the Cross is that God is not remote from our suffering, but knows our pain. Christ joins himself to us in our brokenness, bearing and handling our sorrow. "He was...a man of sorrows, and acquainted with grief... Surely he has borne our griefs and carried our sorrows" (Isaiah 53:3-4).

And so we pray together: O Lord, while so much of life can be joyful and a delight, so much also is grief and loss. We are broken, like poor beggars, lying wounded, isolated and fearful. Our pain is more than we can bear. We have lost much, we hurt today, we sink in darkness. Thank you for those who love and help, and yet we know that you alone can handle the depth of our struggle. Be near me, cling to us, bear our griefs, carry our sorrows. O Lord, teach us to pray. *Amen.*

RENUNCIATION

If any man would come after me, let him deny himself and take up his cross and follow me. —*Mark 8:34*

We have been speaking of "desirable outcomes" in prayer: forgiveness, healing, an end to isolation, hope, consolation. What we are not so eager to hear is that before we can receive any "good" from God, we may need to clear out some space, to shed some of our busyness, some of our stuff, to shake off some attachment. Before there is "joy to the world," we must "prepare him room."

Following Jesus requires that we deny ourselves. Prayer is not just adding more on to an already full life. Prayer will involve subtraction. As Aldous Huxley put it, "Thy kingdom come" means "My kingdom go."

So our prayer must ask honestly and openly about what we need to get rid of, what needs to go. I can do no better on this subject than to let you listen to Thomas Merton:

"The fact remains that contemplation will not be given to those who willfully remain at a distance from God, who confine their interior life to a few routine exercises of piety and a few external acts of worship and service performed as a matter of duty. Such people are careful to avoid sin. They respect God as a Master. But their heart does not belong to Him. They are not really interested in Him, except in order to insure themselves against losing heaven and going to hell. In actual practice, their minds and hearts are taken up with their own ambitions and troubles and comforts and pleasures and all their worldly interests and anxieties and fears. God is only invited to enter this charmed circle to smooth out difficulties and to dispense rewards.

"If a man wants to prepare himself to receive the Holy Ghost and His Love, he must withdraw his desires from all the satisfactions and interests this world has to offer, for spiritual things cannot be appreciated or understood by the mind that is occupied with temporal and merely human satisfactions."

So let us dare to pray together: O Lord, I would prefer to keep my tidy life as is. I shrink back from thinking you would ask me to give up anything at all. But I want to follow Jesus. My world is crammed full, too full for you, so bloated that I cannot maneuver in your direction. Tell me where denial is required. Unhinge me from my dependence on the satisfactions of this world. I want you to have my heart, to have all of me. Along with everyone I know, we want your joy. Prepare that room in me, so I may eagerly pray "Thy kingdom come, my kingdom go." O Lord, teach us to pray. *Amen.*

FEELINGS

*I am weary with my crying. . . . My eyes grow dim with waiting for
my God.* —*Psalm 69:3*

B ut what if I don't feel anything? We may grow anxious about our praying because we miss pious or happy feelings we expected to have when we began to pray. But a little history may lift this burden from our shoulders.

Only in the past century, and only in certain parts of the world, have feelings been regarded as trustworthy measures of whether you are connected to God or not. In fact, for most Christians through most of history, feelings have been viewed suspiciously as untrustworthy. Your feelings may be soaring, you may have warm, fuzzy surges inside you— but this may be simply your personality, or in fact something more dangerous. Martin Luther believed that if we feel good about something, this may be the devil's trickery to seduce us into something contrary to God. Maggie Ross even suggested that an emotional high in prayer may ruin our spirituality, for people may begin to prefer a feeling about God over God!

On the other hand, our feelings may be dark, or even absent. But the saints have always declared (from their own experience—just ask Mother Teresa or Saint Francis) that the most harrowing times, those moments when we feel our emptiest, are the times we are in fact growing toward God. Like the roots of a tall, fruitful tree, living things grow out of the dark.

We need not be surprised when we struggle to feel God's presence, when God seems absent. In a world that is not of God, in a world that is not yet heaven, in our fallible lives, we may expect feelings to come and go.

We may feel God is absent, as did the saints, and prophets—and Jesus himself (when he cried out, "My God, my God, why have you forsaken me?"). But God is not absent, and the secret of the Christian life is developing a consistent life mapped around the God who now seems present, and later seems absent, only to appear more strongly later. Remember that Bonhoeffer said that prayer is finding "the way to God and to speak with him, whether the heart is full or empty." That's what we need.

Certainly if we think about prayer shaping our moral lives, we should be wary of feelings. Too often, morality gets entangled with emotion, and we ask terribly dangerous questions like "Does it feel right?" or "Does it feel good?" Remember: Jesus did not come so we could *feel* different. Jesus came so we could *be* different.

Evelyn Underhill spoke of passing "beyond the need of being fed by mere feeling. . . . [Feelings] are merely the chocolate creams of the Christian life. It is by no means always the perfect lovers who have such feelings. Do not make the mistake of thinking, if you sometimes feel cold and dead, that you do not know how to love."

Prayer is learning how to love, when you are delighting in the chocolate creams, but also when you feel cold and dead.

And so let us pray together: O Lord, sometimes you seem so distant, so remote. I know that part of this is simply who you are, as you are luring us, beckoning to us, out of a world of distractions and confusion. And I confess that part of my sense of your absence is me, my fixation on my way instead of your way. For when I am chasing my own self, I find myself in a cold place. Help me to pass beyond the need for mere feeling. Teach me to love, as you love, as Jesus loved, as I want to love. O Lord, teach us to pray. *Amen.*

THE LIST

Is any one among you suffering? Let him pray. . . . Is any among you sick? Let him call for the elders of the church, and let them pray over him. . . . and the prayer of faith will save the sick man, and the Lord will raise him up; and if he has committed sins, he will be forgiven. Therefore confess your sins to one another, and pray for one another, that you may be healed. —James 5:13-16

When we hear about a friend, a neighbor, or a Church member who is sick or suffering, we wonder, "What can I do?" Always, every time, a profound, tender, eloquent deed of love is quite simply to pray. Prayer is love.

Many Christians, even those who normally are fairly disorganized, maintain a "prayer list." I keep mine in my computer where I can easily add and delete names. Some are permanent (like my sister); others may be there only for a while (like people affected by a recent natural disaster). Some I know well (my children); others I've never met (like a missionary our church supports).

In the words of the old hymn, "What a fellowship!" Not that God is more likely to answer a higher number of prayers—but we are genuinely in community, in "family," with brothers and sisters who daily join hands invisibly in love and prayer, across continents, across the street.

What can we do? We pray, and we may let others know we are praying. Sometimes I get a note that is short, simple, and marvelously encouraging: "I am praying for you."

Our prayer list jogs our memory. Our prayer list is a discipline good for our own souls. Our prayer list lifts us out of zeroing in on ourselves and our concerns and turns us outward with some profound centrifugal force into loving our neighbors, into loving the world.

Typically we pray for those who are sick, or for those in grief. But over time our prayer list can be broadened to include other kinds of concerns. We may pray for holiness, for a deeper faith, for peace in the world, for the schools, for our Church, for those who do not know God. We may pray about moral issues, about hunger and racial reconciliation, about family matters.

A prayer list can get too long, to the point that you don't have time to pray for every person and every concern. So stay focused! Stretch yourself to expand your horizons so that you pray for more than just yourself and your concerns, or your family, but for others, for strangers, for the person you're having difficulties with. Nothing moves us toward a happier relationship with someone from whom we are estranged than the simple act of praying for that person.

So, if you don't have a list, get some paper, or use some other mechanism, and start one now. Your Church may maintain a list. You may not know these people—but you are part of the same family! Pray for those on your list *by name.* Over the next few days, work to expand your list to include others, to expand your vision, to deepen your prayer life.

Let us pray: O Lord, teach us to pray. *Amen.*

HEALING (PART 1)

Lord ... only say the word, and my servant will be healed.
—Matthew 8:8

E very now and then we read a study that indicates the positive effects of prayer in controlled tests. In one study, prayed-for coronary patients got well more quickly than the control (unprayed-for) group, who required more ventilatory assistance, antibiotics, and diuretics. I know physicians who have been startled by cures that they can only can only attribute to the power of prayer.

But haven't you pleaded with God for the recovery of a loved one, only to have those prayers fall to the floor, seemingly unanswered? If prayer works, it doesn't seem to work very well, or not very frequently, or not for the one I loved and couldn't imagine living without.

"Does prayer work?" is the wrong question, really. As I suggested in Lesson 8, it's like measuring your marriage by how frequently your spouse does your bidding. The Bible thinks of prayer as love. Prayer is making a conscious connection with God, daring to touch what is incomparably great and good. Prayer is just a relationship, loving and being loved by God. Love wants only to be together, to share hopes and sorrows.

Back in Lesson 7 we read about Madeleine L'Engle and her husband waiting for a biopsy result. Although the cancer was pronounced terminal, she knew her prayers had not been wasted, for prayer is love, and love is never a waste. Prayers for healing put us in relationship with God, without whom we have no hope no matter if there is healing or not. God gathers up all our prayers, like precious pearls.

Why not pray intently for healing? God wants us to pour out our hearts, to deal honestly, courageously, expressing our deepest desires and dreams. If we love someone, we can do no less. We gather up our relationship of love and offer it up into the hands of God. With undying hope, we earnestly plead for a happy outcome. And if and when there is no happy outcome, we bow our heads in humility and join the ranks of those who know what Mark Helprin meant when he said about God: "Being very clever, He has beaten life into a great question that breaks the living and is answered only in death." We may even storm heaven with our questions and even protests. At the end of the day we have surely deepened our fellowship, with God and with each other. We will say more about healing next time.

But for now, let us pray together: O Lord, we see the faces of those who are sick, suffering, even dying. We know you love them even more than we do, hard as that may be to imagine. We pray for healing, for you to intervene, to alter the outcome. We love those we name, and ask that you gather our love to your love in a beautiful necklace of love that we pray will never be broken. Hear us, and answer. O Lord, teach us to pray. *Amen.*

HEALING (PART 2)

*Jacob . . . breathed his last, and was gathered to his people. Then
Joseph fell on his father's face, and wept over him, and kissed him. . . .
And the Egyptians wept for him seventy days.*   —Genesis 49:33–50:3

When followers of Christ join hands there is already a healing. For many, the most unspeakable aspect of suffering is feeling cut off, isolated. Loneliness, though, can be healed through prayer, and through simply showing up. After his wife's death from cancer, C. S. Lewis wrote these poignant words about his anguish:

"No one ever told me that grief felt so like fear. I am not afraid, but the sensation is like being afraid. The same fluttering in the stomach, the same restlessness, the yawning. I keep on swallowing.

"At other times it feels like being mildly drunk, or concussed. There is a sort of invisible blanket between the world and me. I find it hard to take in what anyone says. Or perhaps, hard to want to take it in. It is so uninteresting."

His next remark points the way for us in our ministry of healing: "Yet I want the others to be about me. I dread the moments when the house is empty. If only they would talk to one another and not to me."

When someone we love is grieving, we have this terrible craving to do something, to fix things, to speak some magically effective words that will produce a smile and make everything okay. And yet, in times of real suffering, this is impossible. All we really can do is just show up. Be there. The worst suffering is isolation, feeling cut off. Cardinal Joseph Bernardin, just weeks before his death, wrote about his ministry to cancer sufferers. He suggests that there is a decisive difference between our pain as disciples and the pain known by those who are not the Lord's disciples. The difference is that we suffer in communion with the Lord. All we can do, and strangely enough it is precisely what is needed, is to "be present to [those who hurt], pray with them—become, in effect, a silent sign of God's presence and love."

A few years ago, a friend of mine spent a week at Lourdes, the shrine in France where the Virgin Mary appeared to Bernadette Soubirous, who was just 14 years old, in 1858. Thousands of gallons of water flow there each day, and thousands claim to have been cured in its streams. When my friend returned, I asked her, "Did you see any miracles?" She said, "Oh yes, every day." "Every day? Tell me!" She explained: "Every day at Lourdes, no matter who you are, or where you are from, or what's wrong with you, you are welcomed, and loved."

Jesus healed. But he performed whatever miracles he performed, not to impress anybody with his power, but to teach a lesson. During Jesus' lifetime, plenty of people still got sick, and limped, and suffered, and died. He did not heal everyone. And, at least as far as we know, he rarely healed in private. He healed in front of a crowd, and he always attached a sermon, a point to the miracle.

The "point" in his ministry of healing would not be health and physical well-being, but rather salvation itself. Jesus' miracles are really foretokens of salvation, tantalizing peeks into the glory of God. There is a difference between healing and salvation. Jürgen Moltmann put it well:

"Healing vanquishes illness and creates health. Yet it does not vanquish the power of death. But *salvation* in its full and completed form is the annihilation of the power of death and the raising of men and women to eternal life. In this wider sense of salvation... people are healed not through Jesus' miracles, but through Jesus' wounds; that is, they are gathered into the indestructible love of God."

So let us pray together: Lord, heal us of the pain of isolation—and show us how we can be the answer to our own prayers, to someone else's prayers. For we long for the wider healing of your salvation. O Lord, teach us to pray. *Amen.*

FRUITFULNESS

And when they had prayed, the place in which they were gathered together was shaken; and they were all filled with the Holy Spirit. . . . There was not a needy person among them.   *—Acts 4:31, 34*

Much of our discussion of prayer has been directed toward "holiness," actually to what John Wesley called "inward holiness"—cultivating the spirit, growing our souls deeper into God, seeking purity of heart. We have a desire somewhere in the recesses of our soul to be clean and whole—a God-given urge toward integrity. God sees us, knows us, and we want our minds and our souls to be conformed to God's image, transformed into Christ's likeness. Thomas of Celano, a biographer who knew St. Francis personally, spoke of St. Francis's naïve, startling conformity to Christ:

He was always with Jesus:
Jesus in his heart,
Jesus in his mouth,
Jesus in his ears,

Jesus in his eyes,
Jesus in his hands,
he bore Jesus always in his whole body.

Pursuing this ideal, we pray not only for "inward holiness," but also for "outward holiness." Prayer desires the fruit of service. Mother Teresa identifies the path from prayer to a deeper faith, from that deeper faith to love, and finally reminds us that "the fruit of love is service."

Dorothy Day, the great hero of outward holiness in the twentieth century, once asked, "Does God have a set way of prayer, a way that He expects each of us to follow? I doubt it. I believe some people—lots of people—pray through the witness of their lives, through the work they do, the friendships they have, the love they offer people and receive from people. Since when are *words* the only acceptable form of prayer?"

More humorously, C. S. Lewis unmasked what many of us do: "I am often, I believe, praying for others when I should be doing things for them. It's so much easier to pray for a bore than to go and see him."

Prayer is a call to action. Even when our inward self is soothed in prayer, there is probably hidden in that soothing a call to action. Elie Wiesel once said, "Whenever an angel says 'Be not afraid!' you'd better start worrying. A big assignment is on the way."

So let us pray together, using these words from Lancelot Andrewes, an English bishop from the seventeenth century:

Lord Jesus, I give you my hands to do your work.
I give you my feet to go your way.
I give you my eyes to see as you do.
I give you my tongue to speak your words.
I give you my mind that you may think in me.
I give you my spirit that you may pray in me.

Above all,
I give you my heart that you may love in me,
your Father, and all humankind.
I give you my whole self that you may grow in me,
So that it is you, Lord Jesus,
Who live and work and pray in me.

Amen.

CALL

And he said to them, "Follow me, and I will make you fishers of men."
Immediately they left their nets and followed him. —Matthew 4:19-20

W hen you watch *It's a Wonderful Life,* look for the great scene where Mr. Potter thinks he can buy off George Bailey with a fat salary, the nicest house in town, some new dresses for Mrs. Bailey, and the occasional business trip to New York. George storms out of Potter's office, back to his little building and loan, with little to show for his enormous efforts—except for a wonderful life and a different kind of Bedford Falls.

George doesn't exude much piety in the film, but his decision exemplifies the Christian life. We are called by God; and prayer is about hearing, wrestling with, and responding to that call. God calls us not just to general niceness or to general do-gooding. No, God has some specific something to which I am called, to which you are called. God wants me here and not there. God wants you to do this, and not that. We are called to do something major with our lives (such as deciding whether to be a teacher or a custodian). We are called to do something seemingly smaller within today's schedule (such as reading to our daughter or dropping by a nursing home).

Admittedly, our culture focuses on "career." In a career (or even just a "job"), the goal is more money, a higher rung on the ladder, a bigger office, more plaudits. But a calling is very different. Calling implies a function within the broader community, and in fact, a role in the betterment of the community.

In his journal, Henri Nouwen wrote about his startling decision to leave his tenured faculty position at Harvard to spend the rest of his life caring for severely handicapped adults at Daybreak, a L'Arche community outside Toronto:

"My decision to leave Harvard was a difficult one. For many months I was not sure if I would be following or betraying my vocation by leaving. The outer voices kept saying, 'You can do so much good here. People need you!' The inner voices kept saying, 'What good is it to preach the Gospel to others while losing your own soul?' Finally, I realized that my increasing inner darkness, my feeling of being rejected by some of my students, colleagues, friends and even God, my inordinate need for affirmation and affection, and my deep sense of not belonging were clear signs that I was not following the way of God's spirit. The fruits of the spirit are not sadness, loneliness, and separation, but joy, solitude, and community. After I decided to leave Harvard, I was surprised that it had taken me so long to come to that decision. As soon as I left, I felt so much inner freedom, so much joy and new energy, that I could look back on my former life as a prison in which I had locked myself."

We pray daily, seeking our calling. And we do so with others, knowing that God's call ultimately weaves us beautifully into the fabric of the community. Brother Roger,

founder of Taizé, whose worship and music have transformed churches and countless lives, once said that we
should not pray for an end, but for a society of free men
with Christ. And women. And children.

So let us pray together: O Lord, help me know to what you
are calling me. Open my eyes and ears. Help me read the
signs in my soul. Create a willing spirit in me, for I know
you may be calling me to something very different in my
work, or in the way I do my work, or with the rest of my
life, or even this afternoon, in the next minute. O Lord,
teach us to pray, and to follow. *Amen.*

THE END AND THE BEGINNING

I urge that supplications, prayers, intercessions, and thanksgivings be made for all men . . . that we may lead a quiet and peaceable life, godly and respectful in every way.   —1 Timothy 2:1-2

Weis come at last to the end, which hopefully will be the true beginning. I hope this has been meaningful. More importantly, I hope you are praying!

Remember, there is only one way to pray, and that is to pray. Prayer is so mundane, so practical, and yet at the same time prayer is transcendent, utterly impractical. Prayer is as simple as the next task on your calendar, and yet as complex as offering every corner of your existence and the world up to a God who is all love, sheer mystery, elusive, and all-encompassing.

I would urge you to recall the practicality of discipline in prayer, for if you stick with praying, great fruit will emerge. Paul Waitman Hoon wrote that people "are more likely to be devout because they are made to pray, than to pray because they feel devout." An Armenian prayer goes like this: "Have mercy on this people...bowed down [before You]. Keep them whole, and stamp upon their hearts the posture of their bodies." So bow, make yourself pray—and over time your heart will conform to your body, your passion to your practice.

Not that the practice of prayer is dull rigor. I love what Wendell Berry wrote to his wife, and with imagination we can apply these words to our relationship to our loving God who is always there.

Sometimes hidden from me
in daily custom and in trust,
so that I live by you unaware
as by the beating of my heart,

suddenly you flare in my sight,
a wild rose blooming at the edge
of thicket, grace and light
where yesterday was only shade,

and once again I am blessed, choosing
again what I chose before.

In prayer we choose again what we chose before. We discover God is as close as the beating of our heart, as beautiful as a rose, all grace and light. Prayer forms and shapes us, as we increase the overlap between my mind and the mind of God.

We never master prayer, but we play out our praying as eager amateurs, learning again and again that Catherine of Siena was right when she prayed, "You, eternal Trinity, are a deep sea: the more I enter you, the more I discover, and the more I discover, the more I seek you."

And we never pray alone. Saints, brothers and sisters across the globe, and friends in your own Church family are praying, today—now. And most wonderfully, Jesus prays for us, and with us. Just as Paul spoke of the Spirit in Romans 8:26: "We do not know how to pray as we ought, but the Spirit himself intercedes for us with sighs to deep for words." What comfort. What hope. What a fellowship. What beautiful work.

And so we for the balance of our lives let us pray together, "O Lord, teach us to pray." *Amen.*

WORKS CITED

Introducing Prayer

Sebastian Brock, *The Luminous Eye: The Spiritual World Vision of Saint Ephrem* (Kalamazoo, Mich.: Cistercian, 1992), p. 75.

Lesson 1: Beginning

Hans Urs von Balthasar, *Prayer* (San Francisco: Ingatius Press, 1986), p. 23.

Lesson 2: Closer Than We Think

Satinder Bindra, "Mother Teresa's Letters Reveal Doubts," article on www.cnn.com/World (7 September 2001).

Oscar Romero, *The Violence of Love* (Farmingham, Pa.: Plough Publishing, 1998), p. 131.

Lesson 3: Barriers to Prayer

Henri Nouwen, *With Open Hands* (New York: Ballantine Books, 1985), pp. 3, 7.

Frederick Buechner, *The Sacred Journey* (San Francisco: HarperSan Francisco, 1982), p. 46.

Lesson 4: Coldness

Thomas Merton, *Spiritual Direction and Meditation* and *What Is Contemplation?* (Wheathampstead, England: Anthony Clarke Books, 1975), p. 85.

Lesson 5: Pray as You Can

Frederick Buechner, *Wishful Thinking: A Theological ABC* (New York: Harper & Row, 1973), pp. 85-86.
Susan Howatch, *Absolute Truths* (New York: Ballantine Books, 1996), p. 473.

Lesson 6: Time

John Eudes in *The Genesee Diary* by Henri Nouwen (Garden City, N.Y.: Image Books, 1981), pp. 139-40.

Lesson 7: What Is in Us

C. S. Lewis, *Letters to Malcolm: Chiefly on Prayer* (New York: Harcourt Brace, 1973), p. 22.
Madeleine L'Engle, *Two-Part Invention* (San Francisco: Harper & Row, 1989), pp. 94-95, 185-87.

Lesson 8: Bruised Knuckles

George Buttrick, *Prayer* (Nashville: Abingdon Press, 1977), p. 36.
C. S. Lewis, *The World's Last Night* (New York: Harvest Books, 1960), p. 8.
Guy Gaucher, *The Story of a Life: St. Thérèse of Lisieux* (San Francisco: HarperSanFrancisco, 1993), p. 193.

Lesson 9: The Way to God

C. S. Lewis, *Letters to Malcolm: Chiefly on Prayer* (New York: Harcourt Brace, 1973), p. 22.
Dietrich Bonhoeffer, *Psalms: The Prayer Book of the Bible* (Minneapolis: Augsburg, 1974), pp. 9-11, 14-15.

Lesson 10: Silence

Saint Augustine, *The Confessions* (Garden City, N.Y.: Image Books, 1960), p. 43.
Mother Teresa, *A Simple Path* (New York: Ballantine Books, 1995), p. 7.

Mother Teresa, *Words to Love By* (Notre Dame, Ind.: Ave Maria Press, 1983), p. 40.

Lesson 11: Scripture

Mother Teresa, *Words to Love By* (Notre Dame, Ind.: Ave Maria Press, 1983), p. 40.

Lesson 12: Jesus Prayed the Psalms

Christoph Barth, *Introduction to the Psalms*, trans. R. A. Wilson (New York: Scribner's, 1966), p. 36.

Saint Ignatius, *The Spiritual Exercises of St. Ignatius*, trans. Anthony Mottola (Garden City, N.Y.: Image Books, 1964).

Arnaldo Fortini, *Francis of Assisi*, trans. Helen Moak (New York: Seabury Press, 1981), p. 557.

Robert Coles, *Dorothy Day: A Radical Devotion* (Reading, Mass.: Addison-Wesley, 1987), p. 16.

Lesson 13: Worship

Annie Dillard, *Holy the Firm* (New York: Harper & Row, 1984), p. 58.

Søren Kierkegaard, *Purity of Heart Is to Will One Thing* (New York: Harper, 1948), p. 180-81.

Roland H. Blainton, *Here I Stand: A Life of Martin Luther* (New York: New American Library, 1950), pp. 266-67, 269.

Saint Augustine, book 1 in *On Christian Doctrine* (Indianapolis: Bobbs-Merrill, 1958).

Lesson 14: Saints

Guy Gaucher, *The Story of a Life: St. Thérèse of Lisieux* (San Francisco: HarperSanFrancisco, 1993), p.146.

Thomas à Kempis, *The Imitation of Christ* (New York: Penguin Books, 1952), p. 162.

Lesson 15: Fasting

Richard J. Foster, *Celebration of Discipline* (San Francisco: Harper & Row, 1978), p. 56.

Lesson 16: A Copernican Revolution

Richard J. Foster, *Prayer* (San Francisco: HarperSanFrancisco, 1992), p. 15.
Dietrich Bonhoeffer, *Letters and Papers from Prison*, ed. Eberhard Bethge (New York: Macmillan, 1972), p. 361.
Maggie Ross, *The Fountain & the Furnace: The Way of Tears and Fire* (New York: Paulist Press, 1987), p. 68.
Saint Francis, *Francis of Assissi: Early Documents, vol. 1* (New York: New City Press, 1999), p. 109.

Lesson 17: Praise

Saint Augustine, book 1 of *On Christian Doctrine* (Indianapolis: Bobbs-Merrill, 1958).
Saint Francis, *Francis of Assissi: Early Documents*, vol. 1 (New York: New City Press, 1999), pp. 113-14.
Stanley Ayling, *John Wesley* (Nashville: Abingdon Press, 1980), p. 315.

Lesson 18: Gratitude

Henri Nouwen, *The Return of the Prodigal* (New York: Image Books, 1993), pp. 85-86.

Lesson 19: Confession

C. S. Lewis, *The Weight of Glory* (New York: Macmillan, 1980), pp. 3-4.
James Melvin Washington, ed., *A Testament of Hope: The Essential Writings and Speeches of Martin Luther King, Jr.* (San Francisco: HarperSanFrancisco, 1986), p. 508.

Lesson 20: Not Your Fault

Frederick Buechner, *The Sacred Journey* (San Francisco: HarperSan Francisco, 1982), p. 46.

Lesson 21: Repentance

Catherine of Siena, *Catherine of Siena: The Dialogue*, trans. Suzanne Noffke (New York: Paulist Press, 1980), p. 364.
Book of Common Prayer (New York: Harper and Brothers, 1944), p. 6.

Lesson 22: Forgiveness (Part 1)

John Irving, *The World According to Garp* (New York: Balantine, 1994), pp. 380-81.

Catherine of Siena, *Catherine of Siena: The Dialogue,* trans. Suzanne Noffke (New York: Paulist Press, 1980).

Lesson 23: Forgiveness (Part 2)

Frederich Buechner, *Wishful Thinking* (San Francisco: Harper-SanFrancisco, 1973), p. 33.

Martin Luther King Jr., *Strength to Love* (Philadelphia: Fortress Press, 1981), p. 54.

Lesson 24: Wounds

Thomas Hobbes in *The English Philosophers from Bacon to Mill,* ed. Edwin A. Burtt (New York: The Modern Library, 1939), p. 161.

Henri Nouwen, *Heart Speaks to Heart* (Notre Dame, Ind.: Ave Maria Press, 1985), pp. 20-21, 28.

Dietrich Bonhoeffer, *Psalms: The Prayer Book of the Bible* (Minneapolis: Augsburg, 1970), p. 48.

Lesson 25: Renunciation

Aldous Huxley in Eugene Peterson, *Traveling Light* (Colorado Springs: Helmers & Howard, 1988), p. 168.

Thomas Merton, *Spiritual Direction and Meditation* and *What Is Contemplation?* (Wheathampstead, England: Anthony Clarke, 1975), pp. 90, 93.

Lesson 26: Feelings

Maggie Ross, *The Fountain & the Furnace: The Way of Tears and Fire* (New York: Paulist Press, 1987), p. 71.

Dietrich Bonhoeffer, *Psalms: The Prayer Book of the Bible,* trans. James Burtness (Minneapolis: Augsburg, 1970), pp. 9-10.

Evelyn Underhill, *The Ways of the Spirit* (New York: Crossroads, 1996), p. 602.

Lesson 28: Healing (Part 1)

R. C. Byrd, "Positve Therapeutic Effects of Intercessory Prayer in a Coronary Care Unit Population," *Southern Medical Journal* 81 (1988): 826-29.

Mark Helprin, *A Soldier of the Great War* (New York: Avon Books, 1991), p. 662.

Lesson 29: Healing (Part 2)

C. S. Lewis, *A Grief Observed* (New York: Bantam, 1961), p. 1.

Joseph Cardinal Bernardin, *The Gift of Peace* (Chicago: Loyola Press, 1997), p. 48.

Jürgen Moltman, *The Way of Jesus Christ* (Minneapolis: Fortress, 1993), pp. 108, 110.

Lesson 30: Fruitfulness

Regis J. Armstrong, ed., *Francis of Assisi: Early Documents*, Vol. 1. (New York: New City Press, 1999), p. 283.

Mother Teresa, *Words to Love by* (Notre Dame, Ind.: Ave Maria Press, 1983), p. 44.

Robert Coles, *Dorothy Day: A Radical Devotion* (Reading, Mass.: Addison-Wesley Pub. Co., 1987), p. 28.

C. S. Lewis, *Letters to Malcolm: Chiefly on Prayer* (New York: Harcourt Brace, 1973), p. 66.

Elie Wiesel in Robert McAfee Brown, *Spirituality and Liberation* (Philadelphia: Westminster Press, 1988), p. 136.

Lancelot Andrewes in Evelyn Underhill, *The Ways of the Spirit* (New York, Crossroads, 1990), p. 22.

Lesson 31: Call

Henri Nouwen, *The Road to Daybreak* (New York: Doubleday, 1988), p. 22.

Afterword: The End and the Beginning

Paul Waitman Hoon, *The Integrity of Worship* (Nashville: Abingdon Press, 1971), p. 320.

Armenian Prayer from J. Alan Kay, *The Nature of Christian Worship* (New York: Philosophical Library, 1954), pp. 70-71.

Wendell Berry, *The Selected Poems of Wendell Berry* (Washington, D.C.: Counterpoint, 1998).

Catherine of Siena, *Catherine of Siena: The Dialogue* trans. Suzanne Noffke (New York: Paulist Press, 1980), p. 364.

SCRIPTURE INDEX

INDEX OF QUOTED WRITERS

A GUIDE FOR SMALL GROUPS

By Kenneth H. Carter, Jr.

James Howell offers the readers thirty-one Lessons in learning to practice Christian prayer. A book is of course an individual experience, a conversation between the author and the reader. But reading a book also invites the individual into a community of readers, especially those motivated to learn the art of prayer. Just as the author is in conversation with the saints (historical and contemporary), it will be helpful for the reader to become a part of a dialogue about the important subject of prayer.

Small groups have been important in the history of Christianity. Jesus called a group of disciples; the book of Acts reports the existence of house churches; and small groups went into the desert to live near holy men and women of faith. In later church history, John Wesley organized the early Methodists of eighteenth-century England into class meetings, and Dietrich Bonhoeffer led and taught a group of underground pastors in a resistance movement against the Nazi movement in the middle of the last century.

In our own day, small groups gather in a variety of ways: Sunday school classes, men's and women's groups, mission groups, *Disciple* Bible Study groups, Emmaus Reunion groups, accountability groups, and support groups. As you read *The Beautiful Work of Learning to Pray*, you might consider making this resource the curriculum for a short course in prayer; or you might call forth a new group of persons who might be led to want to explore the spiritual pursuit of prayer.

LEADING A SMALL GROUP

A small group focusing on *The Beautiful Work of Learning to Pray* will need a leader (or a convener, or guide). The leader issues the invitation to the group, establishes the framework by which the participants study and pray together, and helps to create a climate of support and accountability. The following reminders will be important in the formation of the group and its experience:

- Aim for a diverse group of participants: mature Christians and honest seekers, men and women, activists and intellectuals, newcomers to your community and long-time members. Much of the richness of the book lies in its recognition that "there is no one way to pray" (Lesson 5, "Pray as You Can"). If all of the same participants resonate with one way of praying, we will miss the diverse ways God speaks to us in prayer.

112

- Create a climate of comfort and safety in the group. Many persons do not share their experiences with prayer because they do not trust others to listen (for more on this see Dietrich Bonhoeffer, *Life Together*). Others may question the worthiness of the validity of their prayer lives (Lesson 4, "Coldness"). The leader helps to assure the participants that their prayer lives are important to the group. The leader also guides from a posture of humility (Lesson 2, "Closer Than We Think"; Romans 8:26: *"The Spirit helps us in our weakness; for we do not now how to pray as we ought"*). Even the saints recognized that they were beginners in prayer.
- The group may want to keep the discussions confidential. If so, participants will keep the conversation within the confines of the group meeting itself. They may share impressions about the group with others (I am learning a lot; I enjoy the other participants; our leader is helpful, and so forth), but the specifics of individual struggles and concerns will not be shared outside the group.
- The best groups not only offer support; they also hold participants accountable. The leader will want to give specific guidance in reading and reflecting on the book; for example, which Lessons should be read in preparation for the meeting, which exercises might be experienced in the times between gatherings (such as Lesson 15, "Fasting"). We are often more prone to accomplish an exercise (physical or spiritual) when we know that someone is counting on us to fulfill our promise.
- A small group could reflect on this material in three to six sessions. Many individuals who

might be intimidated by groups that meet for one year or two years are more open to short-term commitments. This is, after all, a book on "beginning to pray." Other prayer studies or experiences might flow out of a meaningful short course in prayer.

ORGANIZING THE LESSONS

Your small group might consider either of the two following ways of structuring the group meetings.

Option One (three meetings)

Option Two (six meetings)

For six meetings, take each group meeting and extend it over two gatherings. The breaks are noted within the study guide. In the six-meeting format, the homework for session 1 will become the homework for session 2, and the homework for session 2 will be for session 4. After session 1, ask the individuals to write down the names of the participants and to pray for them. After session 3, ask the participants to say the Lord's Prayer and the Twenty-third Psalm each day, and to memorize them if possible. After session 5, ask the participants to write their own prayers of praise and gratitude to share with the group.

1. Getting Started

After a welcome, ask the participants to read "Introducing Prayer." Then offer the following questions:

- Can you remember an experience of learning to do something (a sport like tennis or baseball, a musical instrument like the piano or guitar, a craft like quilting or an activity like gardening)? Can you describe the process in the way James Howell does in reflecting on learning to play the piano?

- In "Introducing Prayer," the author suggests that "prayer is our pursuit of beauty." Recall an experience of beauty in your own life, and share with the group. Remember to be creative: beauty is found in children, nature, everyday experience, the arts, a skill flawlessly displayed, a word well spoken.

Rather than having individuals respond to these questions verbally, the leader might give participants time to write in a journal about one of the questions and discuss the other one.

The first Lessons have to do with practical matters related to prayer, obstacles to the practice of prayer, and encouragement in establishing new disciplines and habits. Allow participants to speak in general about practical dimensions of their faith, obstacles to their being disciples of Jesus, and sources of encouragement in their spiritual lives. In Lesson 2 ("Closer Than We Think"), Howell confesses that "prayer isn't easy . . . prayer is difficult."

- Share with the group a way in which the practice of prayer has been difficult for you as a leader (the assumption is that all Christians struggle in some way with prayer). This will help the participants to articulate their own challenges and failures in the spiritual life.
- Ask the group to list reasons why prayer might be understood as difficult.
- The apostle Paul writes: *"the Spirit helps us in our weakness; for we do not know how to pray as we ought"* (Romans 8:26). James Howell also notes that *"even the greatest saints of the Church have*

struggled with their prayer life" (Lesson 2). Are these statements consistent with what we often assume about spiritually mature people? Do you find these statements to be surprising or encouraging?

As your group gets started, remind the participants that they are in wonderful company as they begin the practice of prayer, and that they will have companions even as they struggle.

Session Two
or
Sessions Two and Three

When we think of learning a skill, we think of mastering a discipline or series of activities. And while we can learn to pray, the process is the reverse of our usual expectation. In prayer we yield control. The image in *The Beautiful Work of Learning to Pray* (taken from Henri Nouwen) is of the clinched fist (Lesson 3, "Barriers to Prayer"). Howell writes: "Prayer begins when we admit we need help" (Lesson 3). In asking for help we open our hands to receive what God wants to give to us.

- Invite the participants into a prayer exercise. With eyes closed, ask the individuals to clinch their fists, and to visualize something in their lives is difficult, stressful, destructive, or chaotic. After some time in silence (this practice will require a few moments of transition), ask the individuals to place what they have visualized in the hand of Jesus. Then ask them to slowly unclench their fists, and to open them.
- Teach the chorus from the hymn "I Surrender All" to the group. It can be found on page 354 in *The United Methodist Hymnal*.

In the fifth Lesson, Howell makes the following helpful suggestion: "Pray as you can, not as you can't." "There is no one way to pray," he insists, and this Lesson includes various models and contexts for prayer. Ask the participants to read this Lesson silently.

- After the reading has been completed, ask individuals to discuss which way of praying (if any) was most appealing.
- Ask the participants to consider some small beginning in prayer before the next gathering, and to share what this might look like with the group. Again, we are taking small but important steps in the journey.

Ask the group to pray together, saying the words at the conclusion of Lesson 5.

For homework, ask the participants to read Lessons 10 through 15. The Lessons will be most helpful if they are taken one day at a time, but again, the individual can discover a method that is best for her or him.

2. The Settings of Prayer

In the second group meeting, the participants will reflect on several of the Lessons that form the heart of prayer itself. The group will focus on the following Lessons: "Silence" (10); "Scripture" (11); "Jesus Prayed the Psalms" (12); "Worship" (13); "Saints" (14); and "Fasting" (15). These contexts for prayer provide the soil out of which our prayer lives blossom and become a thing of beauty. These Lessons ground us in the basics of what the Christian tradition has taught us about learning to pray. Sometimes we will hear a comment like "we do not have to reinvent the wheel." If there is truth in this statement, it is captured for our purposes in the settings that have helped Christians to learn to pray.

After a welcome, ask participants to read Lesson 10 ("Silence"). Invite them into a period of silence (3-5 minutes). Then ask them to re-read the Lesson, underlining or circling any phrase or sentence that captures their imaginations.

- For discussion: Respond to the author's question, "Why do we fear silence?"
- Ask participants to recall an important experience of silence.

Another context for prayer is Scripture. In prayer, we ask the Holy Spirit to inspire us in our reading, just as the authors of Scripture were inspired. In prayer, we come to writings that offer models for prayer by faithful men and women across the centuries. And in prayer we allow the Scripture to speak words of judgment and grace to us.

- Ask individuals to discuss an important experience of prayer in the Bible
- Consider the following question: How might Scripture correct or shape our ways of praying?

The Psalms have been called a school of prayer. The author makes a strong case for the centrality of the Psalms in the spiritual life. If individuals have access to Bibles, ask them to read their favorite Psalms, or portions of them. If they do not, read the following Psalms (or verses from within them): Psalm 1; Psalm 8; Psalm 22; Psalm 23; Psalm 51; Psalm 90; Psalm 100; Psalm 139.

- Howell discusses a practical way of praying the Psalms. Invite the participants to consider a commitment to pray through the Psalms in some orderly way.

Session Three
or
Sessions Four and Five

The Lessons of corporate worship (13) and the saints (14) remind us that we pray not only by ourselves, but also *with* others. For many readers, worship will be more familiar, the saints less familiar (although there is much interest in them).

- Ask the participants to reflect on the prayers within their weekly worship services. What is said in those prayers? Are they spontaneous or deliberate, oral or written? Are they meaningful? Do they instruct, comfort, or challenge?
- How might the participants prepare for worship in prayerful ways?
- After reading Lesson 14 ("Saints"), ask the group to come to a common definition of a saint. If there is time, ask if anyone has ever known or met a saint whose life could be defined with these words.

The last Lesson for reflection in this session is "Fasting" (15). This is an important and yet neglected spiritual discipline, and is closely related in Scripture to prayer. Read Matthew 6:9-13 (the Lord's Prayer) and Matthew 6:16-18 (instructions on fasting). The author discusses appropriate ways to fast and insights gained from the practice.

- Howell mentions several meanings of fasting. Ask the group to name some of them. Ask if any have ever fasted and to describe the experience.

For homework, ask the participants to pair off and get the phone number or e-mail address of another person in the group. Agree to undertake special attention to one of the settings of prayer, perhaps the Psalms, or fasting, or silence.

Find some specific way to enter into these settings: choosing a group of psalms to pray, setting aside times for silence, or fasting for a day.

In a closing prayer, ask the group to read the Scriptures out loud that form the introductions to each of the Lessons (10 through 15).

3. The Heart of Prayer

In the last group session, focus on the heart of prayer (or what the author calls the "content" of prayer): praise, gratitude, confession, repentance, forgiveness, renunciation (Lessons 17 through 25).

- Ask the group to read Lesson 16 silently. What is the "Copernican revolution" of which the author speaks?
- Ask one group (or individual) to read Lesson 17 ("Praise") silently, and another group (or individual) to read Lesson 18 ("Gratitude") silently. How are these two words or experiences alike? How are they different?
- Invite participants to recall experiences of meaningful praise or profound gratitude in their own lives.

The author writes that "we sin, we keep God at arms' distance (Lesson 19, "Confession"). He then writes, "at the heart of things, confession is about love. The antithesis of sin is not goodness, but love" (Lesson 20, "Not Your Fault").

- Ask participants to describe the meaning and practice of confession in their own words. In light of 1 John 1:8-9, how and why do we deceive ourselves in pretending that we do not sin and have little need for confession?

Conclusion of Session Three
or
Session Six

The way to this new life, a life of love, is through repentance.

- How does the author define repentance?
- Ask the group to pray Thomas Cranmer's words from *The Book of Common Prayer* out loud (Lesson 21). Then ask the participants: What resonates? What offends? What comforts? What convicts?

The latter Lessons touch on forgiveness, the healing of wounds, the denial of self, the relation of prayer to feelings, the making of lists, and the call of God in prayer. Each topic justifies extended conversation. The following questions can help the participants to integrate these matters into their learning:

- How is forgiveness costly, to God and to us?
- How does forgiveness involve a loss of control?
- Why is renunciation essential and also difficult?
- Why would the author place matters like forgiveness and renunciation later in a course on prayer?
- How do prayer lists expand our vision and deepen our spiritual lives?
- Have you ever prayed for the healing of someone? Why? Why not?
- How can prayer be more connected with action?

Ask participants, in closing, to discuss, in pairs, the following:

- Which Lesson has been most meaningful?
- Which practice seems appropriate to undertake in learning to pray?

- Is there a lingering question or confusion about an aspect of beginning to pray?

The book concludes with a Lesson on calling. Ask the participants to say together the words together at the conclusion of Lesson 31 ("Call").

FOR FURTHER LEARNING

The Beautiful Work of Learning to Pray is a wonderful introduction to the reflections on prayer by Christians across time, space, and tradition. The reader would benefit from further exploration into the writings of many of those quoted in the Lessons: C. S. Lewis, Henri Nouwen, Mother Teresa, Oscar Romero, Thomas Merton, Dietrich Bonhoeffer, and Annie Dillard are among them. Farther back in time, are Saint Francis, Martin Luther, John Calvin, and John Wesley. And even further back, there are the Scriptures, particularly the Psalms.